Da Yu Cun

Hi, Da Yu Cun

# 你好，大余村

汪玉成 主编

西泠印社出版社

你好

Da Yu Cun

# 大余村

一年四季 余村等你　　In 大余村

PREFACE
BY CHIEF EDITOR

# 卷首语 | 写给大余村的气味告白

在大余村这个被时光轻抚的地方，我决定写一封特别的气味告白信，让文字带着一丝丝不易察觉的香气，飘进你的心田。

亲爱的大余村:

你好啊!

我站在这片被阳光亲吻过的土地上，深吸一口气，满口满鼻子灌进来的都是一种味——余味。但你要知道，“余味”在这里，可不只是简单的“什么味”。它呀，说得文艺点，是早晨露珠滑过嫩叶时的清新，是午后老猫慵懒晒太阳时的悠闲，更是夜晚星空下，我们围坐一起分享故事的温馨与甜蜜；说得直接点，它是不同的人跟这个地方发生的化学反应所产生的复合型气味，不只是好闻那么简单!

首先要说的必须是自然的味道。开拓绿水青山生态路的几十年，负氧离子散发出的不可言说的气味，就好像给人体输氧。我在这里的村子游荡，闻着的都是那股子淡淡的泥土芬芳和稻草的清香，一阵阵清新脱俗的香气争先恐后地扑面而来。那一刻，我仿佛能听见树叶在低语，看见花朵在微笑，整个世界都变得柔软而温暖。那是家的味道，是安心的味道。

说到食物的味道，大余村简直是个活生生的美食地图！从村口的烧饼，到小巷子里的非遗汤包，还有流行30年的烧烤PK各类年轻的美食，我尝到的每一口食物都是对味蕾的极致诱惑。这些味道，简单却直击心灵，让人回味无穷。

你知道吗？大余村也有时尚和国际的味道哦！那些背着行囊、带着笔记本电脑的数字游民，他们像是一股清新的风，吹进了这些个古老而又年轻的村庄。他们在这里寻找灵感，也带来了外面的故事和味道。一杯手冲咖啡，不仅融合了世界各地的风味，更让大余村与世界紧密相连。

当然啦，青春和淳朴的味道也是这里所不可或缺的。年轻人用他们的热情和创意，为村子注入了新的活力；而老一辈的人们，则用他们的淳朴和善良，守护着这片土地。在这里，没有所谓的“班味”，只有真诚与纯粹。每一次相遇，都是一次心灵的触碰；每一次交流，都充满了温情与理解。

所以呀，大余村，就是这样一个充满魅力的地方。你的余味，是混合了自然、食物、乡村、时尚、国际、青春和淳朴的复杂而又和谐的味道。感谢你，大余村，让我有幸成为你的一部分，让我因气味相投，而写下这纸告白！

最后，你什么时候回复我呢？

爱你的青年

2024年10月

PREFACE
BY CHIEF EDITOR

# A Fragrant Love Letter to Da Yu Cun

In Da Yu Cun,a place caressed gently by time, I'm writing a unique love letter of scents. Let words carry a faint fragrance and reach deeply into your heart.

Dear Da Yu Cun :

Standing on this sun-kissed land, I breathe in deeply and sense a flavor — a lingering aftertaste. But "aftertaste" here is more than a simple taste. Poetically, it's the freshness of morning dew on tender leaves, the leisure of an old cat under the afternoon sunlight, and the warmth and sweetness of gatherings under the starry sky to share tales. To be simpler, it's a complex scent from the chemical reaction between people and this place, far more than just pleasant.

Firstly, it's the fragrance of nature. Decades of ecological cultivation in the lush mountains and clear waters have filled the air with negative oxygen ions, creating an indescribable aroma. As I stroll through the village, the earthy smell of soil and the fresh scent of rice straw greet me. At that moment, I almost hear the leaves whispering and the flowers smiling. The whole world turns soft and warm. It's the scent of home, the smell of reassurance.

When it comes to food,  is a vivid food map. From the sesame cakes at the village entrance, to the intangible cultural heritage steamed soup dumplings in the alleys, and the 30-year-old barbecue competing with trendy foods, every bite tempts my taste buds. These simple yet stirring flavors linger in memory.

Surprisingly,  also has a sense of fashion and international flair. Digital nomads with backpacks and laptops bring new life. A cup of hand-brewed coffee links the village to the world.

The scents of youth and simplicity are essential. The young add vitality, and the old guard the land. Here, there's no dullness, only sincerity. Each encounter touches souls; each exchange brims with warmth.

Da Yu Cun, you're charming. Your aftertaste is a complex harmony of food, nature, life, fashion, and more. Thank you for letting me be part of you and writing this love letter.

Finally, when will you reply?

Your youth
Oct. 2024

# IN 大余村

## 基本信息

大余村不是一个村，而是以余村景区为核心，由天荒坪镇、山川乡、上墅乡 3 个乡镇 24 个村，共同组成的大余村景区。大余村景区辐射面积 245 平方千米。按照“高能级、现代化、国际范”的发展定位，大余村设计了三个发展圈层：小余村乡村现代化样板建设区（4.86 平方千米）、余村省级旅游度假区核心建设区（40 平方千米）、天山上（1 镇 2 乡）延展区（245 平方千米），以 50 倍的空间布局促进区域发展一体化管理、互通共融，致力于打造体现中国式现代化乡村应有风貌的国际山地旅游目的地。

## 气候情况

亚热带季风气候区，四季分明、温暖湿润、光照充足、雨量充沛、无霜期长。春季气温回升快，但气温变化大；夏季高温高湿，多雷阵雨；秋季降温快，秋高气爽；冬季寒冷干燥，少雨雪。

# 交通指南

## 公共交通

乘坐火车至安吉站，然后可选择打车或乘坐公交车前往大余村景区。安吉县城有多条公交线路可到达余村附近，如 216 路、202 路、202A 路、202 夜间路等。余村附近还有 811 路、临安 K5 路、临安 K11 路、592 路等多条公交线路可供换乘。具体线路和站点信息可咨询当地公交公司或查询相关公交 App。

## 自驾

自驾是最为便捷的交通方式之一。游客可以使用导航软件设定目的地，然后按照导航路线前往即可。

## 其他交通方式

在大余村景区内，游客可以租用共享电动车进行游览。这种方式灵活便捷，适合短途出行和景点之间的衔接。共享电动车的租借点通常位于景区入口或游客中心附近，游客可以根据需要选择租借并支付相应的费用。

## Basic Information

Da Yu Cun is not a single village but a scenic area centered around Yucun Village, comprising 24 villages across three townships: Tianhuangping, Shanchuan, and Shangshu, covering a total area of 245 $km^2$. Positioned as "high-energy, modernization, and international flair", Da Yu Cun plans three major development zones: the Xiao Yucun Village Rural Modernization Model Construction Area (4.86 $km^2$), the Yucun Village Provincial Tourism Resort Core Construction Area (40 $km^2$), and the TianShan (one town, two villages) Extension Area (245 $km^2$). With a 50-fold spatial layout, it promotes integrated regional development management, interconnection, and harmony, striving to become an international mountain tourism destination that embodies the ideal landscape of Chinese-style modern villages.

## Climate Conditions

Located in a subtropical monsoon climate zone, it features distinct seasons, warm and humid weather, abundant sunshine, ample rainfall, and a long frost-free period. Spring brings rapid temperature rises with significant fluctuations; summer is hot and humid with frequent thunderstorms; autumn cools down quickly, offering a crisp and clear atmosphere; winter is cold and dry with little snow or rain.

## Transportation Guide

**Public Transport:**

Take a high-speed train or traditional train to Anji Station, then choose to take a taxi or bus to Da Yu Cun Scenic Area. Several bus lines in Anji County can reach Yucun village, such as bus lines : 216, 202, 202A, and 202 Night bus. There are also multiple bus lines near Yucun village for transfers, including : 811, Lin'an K5, Lin'an K11, and 592. Specific routes and stop information can be obtained from the local bus company or checked on the bus App.

**Self-Driving:**

Self-driving is one of the most convenient ways. Visitors can set the destination in the navigation software and follow the route.

**Other Transportation Methods:**

Within Da Yu Cun Scenic Area, visitors can rent electric scooters or shared electric bikes for sightseeing. This flexible and convenient mode is suitable for short trips and connections between attractions. Rental points for electric scooters or shared electric bikes are usually located near the scenic area entrance or the visitor center, where visitors can choose to rent and pay the corresponding fee as needed.

# 大余村的 四季旅行札记

## 春 · 赏[花]

时间：3 月—5 月

春日里，试图在大余村找到一朵花，是再容易不过的一件事儿了。上墅乡田野边肆意生长的油菜花，民宿门口精心栽培的绣球花……是春天最清新的气息。

那时的你——

**耳机里可能在播放：**《这里会长出一朵花》——旅行团乐队

**手里捧着的可能是：**《丰子恺·四季诗画》——丰子恺

## 夏 · 玩 [ 水 ]

时间：6 月—8 月

“扑通”……是谁从桨板上落水……咕噜咕噜……原来是我自己！依山傍水的大余村，水，是夏日的最佳伴侣。

那时的你——

**耳机里可能在播放：**《他夏了夏天》——苏打绿

**手里捧着的可能是：**《阿波罗之杯》——三岛由纪夫

## 秋 · 观 [ 星 ]

时间：9 月—11 月

长这么大头一次见到完整的北斗七星，原来不需要跋山涉水，在天荒坪的草坪上，足矣！

那时的你——

**耳机里可能在播放：**《水星记》——郭顶

**手里捧着的可能是：**《星际旅行日记》——斯坦尼斯瓦夫·莱姆

## 冬 · 滑 [ 雪 ]

时间：12 月—次年 2 月

“当赤道留住雪花”，大余村亦可留住一片雪景，去成全南方人那一份对雪的“我偏要勉强”。

那时的你——

**耳机里可能在播放：**《雪之华》——中岛美嘉

**手里捧着的可能是：**《乞力马扎罗的雪》——欧内斯特·海明威

# *Notes on Four Seasons' Travel in Da Yu Cun*

**Spring • Flower Viewing**

Time: March - May

In the springtime, trying to find a flower in Da Yu Cun is the easiest thing to do. The rapeseed flowers are growing wildly by the fields of Shangshu Village, and the hydrangeas are carefully cultivated at the entrance of the homestays... . They all exude the freshest breath of spring.

At that moment, you— Might have "A Flower Will Bloom Here" by Travel Band playing in your earphones.
Might be holding "Poems and Paintings of the Four Seasons" by Feng Zikai in your hands.

**Summer • Water Play**

Time: June - August

"Splash"... who fell off the paddleboard?... Glug glug... it was me! In Da Yu Cun , nestled by mountains and waters, water is the best companion in summer.

At that moment, you— Might have "Summer Has Come" by Sodagreen playing in your earphones.
Might be holding "The Cup of Apollo" by Mishima Yukio in your hands.

**Autumn • Star Gazing**

Time: September - November

For the first time in my life, I saw the complete Big Dipper without having to travel far. On the lawn of Tianhuangping, it's enough!

At that moment, you — Might have "Mercury Records" by Guo Ding playing in your earphones.
Might be holding "Interstellar Travel Diary" by Stanisław Lem in your hands.

**Winter • Snow Play**

Time: December - February of the next year

"When the equator retains snowflakes", can also retain a snowy landscape, fulfilling the southerners' longing for snow, "I insist on having it."

At that moment, you— Might have "Snowflower" by Mika Nakashima playing in your earphones.
Might be holding "The Snows of Kilimanjaro" by Ernest Hemingway in your hands.

# 来大余村不得不知道的一些"名词解释"

## 1.余村（世界最佳旅游乡村）

余村地处天目山中国大竹海碧波荡漾之中，由山、水、林、田、湖、草等自然资源构成生命共同体。景区、度假村、民宿（农家乐）、漂流、旅游商品，是余村重要的旅游资源。余村也全力打造践行“绿水青山就是金山银山”理念的实践示范村，建设中国最美县域的新农村样板村。

## 2.余村全球合伙人

深刻认同、积极践行、广泛传播“绿水青山就是金山银山”理念和可持续发展理念，在大余村合作创办企业、开展投资、研发创新或参与服务活动，与余村共担风险，共历艰辛，共建品牌，共创模式，共享未来的海内外绿色发展企业、机构与人才。

### 3．“青来集”青年人才社区

“青来集”名称取自“一水护田将绿绕，两山排闼送青来”。它不仅是空间上的集结和聚集，更是容纳青年一起寻找与成长的共情、激发志同与道合的共振的理想场域，一个让青年在更大世界寻找崭新答案的理想之地。

### 4．DN 余村

DNA（安吉数字游民公社）创始团队在余村创立的新数字游民方舟。DN 余村拥有 7188 平方米的室内面积，由 A、B 两个相邻的独立空间组成，空间内包括 51 间客房（15 个多人间，36 个单人间和双人间），超过 4000 平方米的联合工作空间。

### 5．$O_2$ 生态文化圈

$O_2$ 生态文化圈计划以全域生态与人文资源为青年活力生态营造场景，以品牌 IP 活动、时尚生活方式场景构建青年在村社交矩阵，以青年共创行动、青年社群活动组建青年在村同频价值社区，营造当代青年在村可持续生活方式。

### 6．青年在村

大余村一种全新的生活方式——来自全球各地的青年积极参与乡村建设，打破城乡、年龄的藩篱，为乡村注入新活力和创造力。

### 7．大自然工位

大自然工位是大余村青年人才社区所提倡的一种新兴的工作方式，将大余村内的山、水、林、田、湖等自然资源与文化礼堂、咖啡馆、民宿、“青来集”等各类空间整合打造成余村大自然工位，营造一个充满活力、创造力和生命力的自由办公创业场域。

## *Here are some essential " term explanations " you must know*

**Yucun Village (The World's Best Tourism Village)**

Yucun Village, in the China Bamboo Sea of Tianmu Mountain, forms a life community with mountains, waters, etc. natural resources. It's tourism resources include scenic spots, resorts, etc. Yucun Village aims to be a model village for practicing "lucid waters and lush mountains are invaluable assets" concept and a new rural model in the most beautiful county.

**Yucun Village Global Partnership Program**

Domestic and foreign green enterprises, institutions, and talents, who recognize and spread "lucid waters and lush mountains are invaluable assets" and sustainable development concepts, cooperate in Da Yu Cun for business, investment, R & D, or service. They share risks, build brands, create models, and future with Yucun Village.

**[Youth to Rally] Youth Talents Community**

It's not just a spatial gathering. It's a place for young people to feel empathetic growth, resonate with like - minded peers, and seek new answers in a wider world.

## DN Yucun Village

DN Yucun Village is a new digital nomad ark established by the founding team of DNA (Anji Digital Nomad Commune) in Da Yu Cun Village. It boasts an indoor area of 7,188 square meters, comprising two adjacent independent spaces, A and B. Within these spaces, there are 51 rooms (15 dormitories, 36 single and double rooms), and a co-working space spanning over 4,000 square meters.

## Youth in the Village

A new lifestyle in Da Yu Cun — young people from around the world actively participate in rural development, breaking down barriers of urban-rural divide and age, and injecting new vitality and creativity into the village.

## $O_2$ Eco-cultural Circle

The $O_2$ Eco-cultural circle plan uses regional resources to create youth - friendly ecological scenes. It builds a village social matrix via brand activities and lifestyle scenes, a value community through co - creation and community activities, aiming for a sustainable youth village lifestyle.

## Nature Workspace

Advocated by the Youth Talent Community, it combines Da Yu Cun's natural resources with cultural halls, cafes, homestage etc. to create nature workstations, forming a vibrant office and entrepreneurial area.

# 大余村，是一张世界地图

## 安吉“小瑞士”——江南天池

江南天池四季如画，春天山花烂漫，云雾缭绕；夏季凉风入怀，月盘如玉；秋天树叶斑驳，云海缥缈；冬季银装素裹，雪洁冰晶。漫步其中，偶遇天池旁的欧式城堡，让人恍如穿越到了瑞士一角。

## 住在“土耳其”——云上草原 1168 星空天文酒店

酒店的房间设计借鉴了土耳其洞穴酒店的风格，采用错落复式的空间布局，以及原始洞穴的设计灵感，内部装饰以星空、树屋、洞穴等元素为主，营造出一种奇幻而舒适的氛围。

## “新西兰”牧场——云上草原霍比特人村

云上草原霍比特人村内的霍比特人小屋是景点的核心亮点，小屋仿照电影《霍比特人》和《指环王》中的建筑风格，采用低矮、圆润的设计。一眼望去，绿色的草原、小巧的拱门和篱笆围栏，一派新西兰风格自然风光。

## 相约“巴厘岛”——瀑布咖啡

瀑布咖啡（巴厘岛版）融入了浓郁的热带风情元素，装饰风格独特，充满了异国情调，置身其中，仿佛置身于遥远的巴厘岛。

## “摩洛哥”风情——H2 角头街区酒吧

酒吧的主体外墙被粉刷成鲜艳的橘红色，这种摩洛哥风格的设计不仅为村子带来了更多活力，也成了游客眼中的一道亮丽风景线。

# *Da Yu Cun,*
# *A World Map*

**Anji's "Little Switzerland" — Jiangnan Tianchi**

Jiangnan Tianchi is picturesque in all seasons. Strolling through, one might chance upon a European-style castle beside the lake, creating an illusion of stepping into a corner of Switzerland.

**Staying in "Turkey" — Star Astronony Hotel Of Skyland**

The room design of this hotel draws inspiration from the cave hotels in Turkey, adopting a staggered duplex spatial layout and design concepts inspired by primitive caves. The interior decoration revolves around elements like the starry sky, treehouses, and caves, crafting a whimsical yet cozy ambiance.

**"New Zealand" Ranch — Hobbit Village Of Skyland**

The Hobbit holes within Sky Land Hobbit Village are the core attraction. These huts mimic the architectural style seen in the movies "The Hobbit" and "The Lord of the Rings," characterized by their low, rounded designs.

**Meeting in "Bali" — Waterfall Coffee**

Waterfall Coffee (Bali Version) infuses rich tropical elements into it's decor, exuding an exotic charm that transports visitors to the distant shores of Bali.

**"Moroccan" Charm — H2 Jiaotou Street Bar**

The bar's exterior is painted in a vibrant tangerine hue, embodying Moroccan design that injects more vitality into the village and becomes a striking visual attraction for tourists.

# 很高兴
# 你也喜欢艺术

## 余村邮局

余村邮局是当地青年文创与中国邮政合作的新产物，是“绿水青山就是金山银山”理念诞生地安吉余村的新地标，内里还有农文创产品展销区，展示和销售当地青年自主设计的文创产品以及安吉特色农产品，如以生态之绿为主题的文创产品等。

✉ 天荒坪镇余村

## 青年在村生活灵感便利店

由青年在村创业的文创店，原本是村民售卖当地特产的店铺，后被改造成一家充满创意和温暖氛围的便利店，内里有许多余村数字游民设计的文创产品。

✉ 天荒坪镇余村

## 余村后巷

余村后巷原本是余村村民宅间的一条原汁原味的普通巷子，随着越来越多的全球合伙人项目的入驻，在新业态不断涌现的同时，它逐渐成为一个“新老融合·生活共创·精神共富”的乡村新空间。

✉ 天荒坪镇余村

## 格物长然艺术部落

格物长然艺术部落的成立为山川乡的艺术乡建工作注入了新的活力，推动了更多艺术元素融入乡村景观和文旅项目。艺术部落内还有用于展示各种主题艺术雕塑作品的雕塑展览馆，为村民和游客提供了一个欣赏艺术的新去处。

✉ 山川乡高家堂村

## 竹境 • 竹文化街区

竹境 • 竹文化街区是由 5 个形态各异的原竹建筑组成的步行街区，既有竹建筑模型馆、竹文化书吧等竹文化特色业态，也有茶饮、咖啡、烧烤、轻食等旅游业态，是上墅打造的乡村版竹文化特色街区。

✉ 上墅乡刘家塘村

*I'm glad you also love art!*

**Yucun Post Office**

Yucun Post Office is a new product of the cooperation between local youth cultural creativity and China Post.There is an exhibition and sales area for agricultural cultural and creative products, showcasing and selling locally designed cultural and creative products by young people as well as special agricultural products from Anji.

Address: Yucun Village, Tianhuangping Town

**Youth's Life Inspiration Convenience Store in Rural Areas**

Originally a shop where villagers sold local specialties, it has been transformed into a convenience store filled with creativity and warmth. Inside, you can find many cultural and creative products designed by digital nomads in Yucun Village.

Address: Yucun Village, Tianhuangping Town

### Yucun Village Back Alley

Yucun Village Back Alley was originally an ordinary alley that retained the authentic charm of the villagers' homes in Yucun Village. With the increasing number of global partnership projects settled in, and the continuous emergence of new business forms, it has gradually transformed into a new rural space that combines "old and new, co-creation of life, and shared spiritual wealth."

Address : Yucun Village, Tianhuangping Town

### Gewu Changran Art Tribe

The establishment of the Gewu Changran Art Tribe has injected new vitality into the art-based rural revitalization efforts in Shanchuan Township, promoting the integration of more artistic elements into rural landscapes and cultural tourism projects.

Address: Gaojiatang Village, Shanchuan Township

### Zhujing • Bamboo Cultural Street

It features bamboo-themed businesses such as bamboo architecture model museums, bamboo cultural book bars, as well as tourism-related businesses like tea shops, cafes, barbecue, and light meals.

Address: Liujiatang Village, Shangshu Township

# 人文！人文！

## 姚家大院

姚家大院由姚姓徽商（姚斯侯）所建，是明清时期的私家园林建筑。

级别：省级文物保护单位

⊠ 天荒坪镇井村村

## 两山会址

“绿水青山就是金山银山”理念的诞生地、见证地和纪念地，也是进行党史学习教育、社会主义生态文明教育的重要场所。

级别：浙江省第一批革命文物

⊠ 天荒坪镇余村村文化礼堂二楼

## 新四军苏浙军区第三次反顽战役前线指挥部旧址

在新四军苏浙军区第三次反顽战役中发挥了重要作用。

级别：浙江省第一批革命文物

✉ **天荒坪镇马吉村吴家道自然村**

## 三庆桥

三庆桥是一座清代建筑，具有悠久的历史和独特的建筑风格。

级别：县级文物保护单位

✉ **山川乡船村村**

## 阮氏古宅

阮氏古宅作为近现代重要史迹及代表性建筑，展现了民国时期建筑风格和当地民居特色。

级别：县级文物保护单位

✉ **山川乡大里村**

## 石佛寺石刻

石佛寺石刻是石窟寺及石刻类文物，具有较高的艺术价值和历史价值。

级别：县级文物保护单位

✉ **山川乡马家弄村毛坞塘**

# Humanities and History

### Yao Family Courtyard

Yao Family Courtyard was built by Yao Sihou, a Huizhou merchant surnamed Yao, and was a private garden architecture from the Ming and Qing dynasties.

Level: Provincial-level Cultural Relic Protection Unit.

Address: Jingcun Village, Tianhuangping Town

### Site of the Two Mountains Theory

This is the birthplace, witness, and commemorative site of the Two Mountains theory, and also an important place for learning about party history and socialist ecological civilization education.

Level: First Batch of Revolutionary Cultural Relics in Zhejiang Province

Address: Second Floor of the Cultural Center, Yucun Village, Tianhuangping Town

### Former Site of the Front Command of the New Fourth Army's Jiangsu-Zhejiang Military Region's Third Anti-Reactionary Campaign

This site played a crucial role during the third anti-reactionary campaign of the New Fourth Army's Jiangsu-Zhejiang Military Region.

Level: First Batch of Revolutionary Cultural Relics in Zhejiang Province

Address: Wujiadao Natural Village, Maji Village, Tianhuangping Town

## Sanqing Bridge

Sanqing Bridge is an ancient architectural structure from the Qing Dynasty, featuring a long history and unique architectural style.
Level: County-level Cultural Relic Protection Unit
Address: Chuancun Village, Shanchuan Township

## Ruan's Residence

As an important historical site and representative architecture from modern times, Ruan's Residence showcases the architectural style of the Republic of China period and the local folk residence characteristics.
Level: County-level Cultural Relic Protection Unit
Address: Dali Village, Shanchuan Township

## Stone Carvings of Shifo Temple

The stone carvings of Shifo Temple are cultural relics of grotto temples and stone carvings, possessing high artistic and historical value.
Level: County-level Cultural Relic Protection Unit
Address: Maowutang, Majianong Village, Shanchuan Township

大余村
文旅手绘地图
cultuval and tourism hand-drawn maps
图例
乡镇
村庄
酒店•民宿
餐饮
古建
寺庙
景区
业态
民艺
大麓书院
拾木工坊
化度寺
上墅村
上墅乡
竹境
青年在村生
余村印象青年图书馆
长歌行餐厅
施阮村
美在余村
原力山谷
龙王村
龙王古道群
江南天池
董岭花灯
董岭村

星潮营地
南屿茶事
井村
姚家大院
余村烧饼
吴均汤包
乡音小馆
山河村
青来集
天荒坪镇
天荒坪烧烤一条街
横路村
南屿山露营地
中国大竹海
天下银坑
云上草原
竹马灯
鳌鱼灯
石佛寺
H2角头街区咖啡酒吧
马家弄村
山川乡
山川村
云下湖畔·水上运动基地
灵溪山风景区
高家堂村
格物长然艺术部落
IN·竹野躺平基地
大里村
大溪村
藏龙百瀑
熊猫部落
阮氏古宅
瀑布咖啡（巴厘岛版）
井空里峡谷
船村
璞拉那
九亩村
金钱松国家森林公园

CONTENT

# 目 录 |

你好，大余村
HI , Da Yu Cun

## 卧虎藏龙
## Crouching Tiger, Hidden Dragon

## 云上天空
## Live In Skyland



## 户外山野
## Outdoor Wilderness

## 青年在村
## Youth in the village

## $O_2$ 生态文化圈

## $O_2$ Eco-Cultural Circle

## 人文弧光
## Splendid Humanities

## 玩转四季
## The Beauty of Four Seasons



## 饮居岁月
## Accommodation and meals

Da Yu Cun

# 你好，大余村

# 余村"两山"景区

“绿水青山就是金山银山” 理念诞生地，也是联合国世界旅游组织认证的 “世界最佳旅游乡村” 和全国首个五星级地质文化村。联合国前副秘书长、联合国环境规划署前执行主任索尔海姆来到余村有感而发，表示他在安吉等地看到的，“就是未来中国的模样，甚至是未来世界的模样。”

## Yucun Village " Two Mountains " Scenic Area

It is the birthplace of the concept that "lucid waters and lush mountains are invaluable assets", and it is also a "Best Tourism Village" certified by the United Nations World Tourism Organization and the first five-star geological culture village in China. Eric Solheim, former Deputy Secretary - General of the United Nations and former Executive Director of the United Nations Environment Programme, was inspired when he visited Yucun. He said that what he saw in Anji "is the look of future China and even the look of the future world."

# 中国大竹海

国家 AAAA 级旅游景区，中国东南部的竹文化生态休闲旅游区，浙江省著名的大毛竹示范基地，有着“中国毛竹看浙江，浙江毛竹看安吉，安吉毛竹看港口” 之誉，也是奥斯卡获奖影片《卧虎藏龙》的取景地。

## Great Bamboo Sea of China

A national AAAA scenic spot, it is the largest bamboo cultural eco-leisure tourism area in southeastern China and the most famous giant bamboo demonstration base in Zhejiang Province. It was also the filming Address for the Oscar-winning film "Crouching Tiger, Hidden Dragon".

# 云上草原

2023 年入选中国体育旅游精品项目的综合性特色山地自然风景区，有 “云上一天，草原四季” 的美誉，这里坐拥稀缺高山自然资源和云海奇观。

## The Skyland

Selected as a featured mountain natural scenic area for China's sports tourism boutique projects in 2023, it enjoys the reputation of "One day on the cloud, four seasons on the grassland." This place boasts rare high-mountain natural resources and spectacular sea of clouds.

# 天荒坪<br>抽水蓄能电站<br>（江南天池）

天荒坪抽水蓄能电站是我国首批大型抽水蓄能电站之一，也是亚洲第一、世界第二大抽水蓄能电站，上下水库落差607米，承担着华东电网调峰、调频、事故备用等任务。其上水库即著名的江南天池，为国家AAAA级旅游景区。

## Tianhuangping Pumped Storage Power Station (Jiangnan Tianchi)

Tianhuangping Pumped Storage Power Station is one of the first batch of large pumped storage power stations in China. It is also the largest pumped storage power station in Asia and the second largest in the world. The elevation difference between the upper and lower reservoirs is 607 meters. It undertakes tasks such as peak regulation, frequency modulation and emergency reserve for the East China Power Grid. It's upper reservoir is the famous Jiangnan Tianchi, which is a national AAAA-level tourist scenic area.

# 云上天路

“云上天路”是串联天荒坪镇、上墅乡、山川乡三个乡镇的纽带，约 24 千米长。建成后将成为余村大景区的主要交通走廊，为打造“高能级、现代化、国际范”大余村夯实硬件基础，全面提升大余村承载能力。

## Cloud Skyway

"Cloud Skyway" is a 24-kilometer link connecting Tianhuangping Town, Shangshu Township, and Shanchuan Township. Upon completion, it will become the main transportation corridor of the Da Yu Cun scenic area, and lay a solid hardware foundation for building Da Yu Cun into a high-level, modern and internationally renowned village, and comprehensively enhance the carrying capacity of Da Yu Cun.

# 长龙山抽水蓄能电站

地处华东电网负荷中心，厂房内共布置6台35万千瓦抽水蓄能机组，总装机容量210万千瓦，是华东地区重要的抽水蓄能电站与电网调节电源。

## Changlongshan Pumped Storage Power Station

Located in the load center of the East China Power Grid, the powerhouse is equipped with six 350,000-kilowatt pumped storage units, with a total installed capacity of 2.1 million kilowatts. It is the important pumped storage power station and grid regulation power source in East China.

# 白茶祖

白茶祖是位于天荒坪镇大溪村海拔800余米处的一株百年以上树龄的珍稀白茶树，它是安吉白茶的起源，被立碑纪念，称为“白茶祖”，所产安吉白茶获有“国家地理标志产品”等多项荣誉。

## White Tea Ancestor

The White Tea Ancestor is a rare white tea tree over 100 years old, located at an altitude of over 800 meters in Daxi Village, Tianhuangping Town. It is the origin of Anji white tea and has been commemorated with a monument as the "Ancestor of White Tea",and Anji white tea has been granted honors including the "National Product of Geographical Indication" status as well as many other awards.

# 理查德·克莱德曼国际音乐会

理查德·克莱德曼国际音乐会于2024年7月8日在余村余山矿坑遗址举行，这是其2024中国巡演的首场户外演出。这位拥有267张金唱片和70张白金唱片、获金钢琴奖等诸多荣誉的钢琴大师，用音乐为中法建交60周年献上特殊礼物，促进了中法文化交流。

## Richard Clayderman International Concert

The Richard Clayderman International Concert was held at the Yushan Mine Pit Site in Yucun Village on July 8th,2024.He presented a special gift to the 60th anniversary of the establishment of diplomatic relations between China and France through music, promoting cultural exchange between China and France.

# 秋果艺术节

2024 安吉秋果艺术节于 9 月 14 至 17 日于天荒坪镇余村印象大草坪举办，以现场音乐、脱口秀等精彩活动编织起一场艺术盛宴，为人们带来了一场沉浸式的视听与心灵的美好旅程。

## ChillGo Art Festival

2024 ChillGo Art Festival was held on the lawn of Yucun Village Impression in Tianhuangping Town from September 14th to 17th 2024.With wonderful activities such as Livehouse and talk shows, it wove an artistic feast, bringing people an immersive and wonderful journey for both audio-visual enjoyment and spiritual experience.

# “两山”山地户外运动多项赛

山川乡举办的省级品牌赛事，已连续举办六年，其巧妙串联自然景观，展现文体旅融合魅力。自举办以来，规模和影响力持续扩大，是山川乡打造的文体旅融合“金名片”之一。

## " Two Mountains"
## *Mountain Outdoor Multi - Sport Competition*

A provincial-level brand event held in Shanchuan Township for six consecutive years, cleverly connects natural landscapes and showcases the charm of sports and tourism integration.

# 青年人才社区

“青来集”是荣获 2024 年度营商环境优化提升“最佳实践案例”的乡村版青年人才社区，吸引众多青年人才入驻，推动当地乡村振兴。

## Youth Talents Community

Youth to Rally is a rural youth talent community that won the "Best Practice Case" award for optimizing and improving the business environment in 2024.

# 安吉（余村）生态文明国际传播中心暨国际传播平台观察点

2024年3月，安吉（余村）生态文明国际传播中心暨国际传播平台观察点在余村“青来集”成立。同年11月，在此基础上，安吉生态文明国际传播研究中心在余村印象成立，旨在实现生态文明故事的全球化表达，持续展示湖州、安吉的国际形象。

## *Anji(Yucun Village) Eco-Civilization International Communication Center and International Communication Platform Observation Point*

In March 2024, Anji(Yucun Village) Eco-Civilization International Communication Center and International Communication Platform Observation Point was established in "Youth to Rally" Youth Talents Community. In November of the same year, the International Communication Research Center for Ecological Civilization was established in Yucun Village Impression.

# 卧虎藏龙

Crouching Tiger , Hidden Dragon

一根竹子，从盘根错节中挣脱，融入日月山川，
成为一道宏大的风景。我便看见了海的辽阔以及山的悠远。

Within the endless bamboo forest, I caught sight of the vastness of the sea and the remoteness of the mountains.

# 江南意境里亦有 **大开大合**

文 / 刘林

人们常说江南是温婉的，大余村自然也不例外。小桥、流水、炊烟、人家……这些很是常见，并不稀缺。但安吉是竹乡，换句话说，大余村有着太多竹了。

竹承载了诸多令人向往的美好品格，且无一例外都是极具风骨的：竹与梅、兰、菊并称“四君子”，又与梅、松合称“岁寒三友”，是坚韧；它身形挺直，宁折不弯，是正直；它外直中通，虚怀若谷，是谦卑；它虽有竹节，却不止步，是进取。

因着竹的风骨与气势，大余村山山水水的温婉里又怎么能不藏着锋芒，不藏着大开大合之势？甚至不用“藏”，它们就在那儿，你走近，便能感受到。

Tips

**| 竹·中国大竹海**

中国大竹海景区内山峦起伏，竹林茂密，浩瀚无边，蓝天白云下，竹浪翻滚，宛如仙境，是多部著名影视作品的拍摄地。在这里，还可以参与观竹王、望竹海、嬉竹泉、赏竹艺等多种活动，感受竹文化的深厚底蕴。

✉ 天荒坪镇五鹤村

## | 水 · 藏龙百瀑

藏龙百瀑是浙江最大的瀑布群，拥有大小瀑布 100 多处。景区内著名景点有“长龙飞瀑”、“虹贯龙瀑门（人称小黄果树瀑布）”等。景区所在地曾是太平军的一个据点。据史料记载，19 世纪中叶，忠王李秀成率领的太平军曾在此地演绎了一场“长毛战清妖”的英雄故事。后为纪念太平天国将士的英雄业绩，改长龙山为太平天国“小梁山”。

✉ 天荒坪镇

## Ⅰ道·龙王古道

龙王古道在上墅乡，包含阴山、东坞大岭、回峰岭、欢喜岭、蓑衣塘古道 5 条分支，砌筑于明清时期，人文底蕴深厚。古道路面由块石铺筑，山体陡峭，时宽时窄，平缓时平铺，陡峭处有台阶。沿途青山叠翠如画，有茂林修竹、飞湍瀑流、鸟鸣山幽等自然景观，有小桥流水人家，还有丰富的人文古迹，如花竹、闽省义冢、点将石等。

🖂 上墅乡龙王村

## Ⅰ山·井空里大峡谷

井空里大峡谷是一处免费的自然景区，游客无须购买门票即可进入游览。这里以跌宕起伏的峡谷风光著称，峡谷间水潭密布、错落有致。景区内的溯溪线路适合不同难度需求的户外探险爱好者。对于喜欢徒步的游客来说，这里也是一处不错的徒步胜地。

🖂 山川乡双水线

## *In the picturesque Jiangnan, there's also grandeur and openness.*

People often say Jiangnan is gentle and elegant, and Da Yu Cun is no exception. Small bridges, flowing water, cooking smoke, and homes... these are common sights and not rare at all. However, Anji is the land of bamboo. In other words, Da Yu Cun has an abundance of bamboo.

Bamboo embodies many admirable qualities, all of which are marked by elegance and strength: Bamboo is known as one of the "Four Gentlemen" along with plum, orchid, and chrysanthemum, and as one of the "Three Friends of Winter" with plum and pine, representing resilience; it stands tall and straight, bending but never breaking, embodying integrity; it's exterior is straight, but it's interior is open, symbolizing humility; and although it has joints, it never stops growing, representing progress.

Because of bamboo's strength and grandeur, how could Da Yu Cun's otherwise gentle landscapes not hide a sharp edge? How could it not carry a spirit of boldness and expansiveness? It doesn't even need to hide them—they are right there, and as you approach, you can feel them.

## Tips:

**The Great Bamboo Sea of China** in Tianhuangping Town is the filming address of many famous film and television works. Here, you can participate in various activities and experience the profound heritage of bamboo culture.
**Address:**Wuhe Village, Tianhuangping Town

**Hidden Dragon Waterfall** in Tianhuangping Town is Zhejiang's largest waterfall group with over 100 waterfalls. It includes "Long Dragon Waterfall" and "Rainbow Through the Dragon Gate" .The area has historical significance related to the Taiping Army.
**Address:**Tianhuangping Town

**Longwang Ancient Trail** in Shangshu Township comprises five branches with profound cultural heritage. It's surrounded by luxuriant trees, bamboo groves, waterfalls, and picturesque scenery.
**Address:**Longwang Village, Shangshu Township

**Jingkongli Grand Canyon** in Shanchuan Township is a free natural scenic area known for it's dramatic canyon landscapes and clear pools. It offers varying difficulty levels for river tracing and is excellent for hiking.
**Address:**Shuangshui Line, Shanchuan Township

# 银幕竹海生活

文 / 樊多多

2000年是一个新千年的序幕，就音乐和电影而言，这一年的星光璀璨足以让人们从多重角度记住“千禧年”。而对于偏安一隅的安吉而言，北上广深的观众在《卧虎藏龙》的竹林斗剑场景里看到，并记住了“安且吉兮”的美好之地。666.7万平方米的竹海是电影要传达的东方美学意境的重要元素，一部在当年唯一获得奥斯卡最佳外语片奖项的华语电影，重塑了西方观众对东方文化与价值的想象。

一片中国大竹海承得起刀光剑影和侠骨柔情，也包容得下人间冷暖、诗与远方。《像雾像雨又像风》《白蛇传说》《蜗居》等影视佳作让更多人的目光聚焦到安吉。竹海、乡村、自然意趣，银幕之中、故事之外，观众收获了向往的生活的样子，于是从银幕到生活，越来越多的人与安吉大余村产生了联系。

五鹤村、银坑村、姚家大院；中国大竹海、江南天池。人生如戏，戏如人生。漫步在这些银幕中的故事发生地，邂逅一部影视作品便仿佛跨越时空与那些人物对话，也许一转身便进入一个场景，于是自己也入了戏。

## Tips

跟着电影游大余村，可以有如下选择：天荒坪镇五鹤村的中国大竹海景区，是电影《卧虎藏龙》、电视剧《像雾像雨又像风》的拍摄地；天荒坪镇的江南天池景区是电影《飞驰人生》的拍摄地；天荒坪镇银坑村是《夜宴》《心中有鬼》等电影的拍摄地；天荒坪镇井村的姚家大院是电视剧《成长》的拍摄地。除了体验影视文化，在村与村之间来一场Country Walk，说不定会有意外惊喜。

## *On Screen, Bamboo Forest, and Life*

The year 2000 marked the dawn of a new millennium. As for music and film, the brilliance of that year was enough to make people remember the "millennium" from multiple perspectives. For Anji, a quiet corner of China, the audience in cities like Beijing, Shanghai, Guangzhou, and Shenzhen saw and remembered the beautiful "AnJi" through the iconic bamboo forest sword-fight scene in Crouching Tiger, Hidden Dragon. The 666.7-hectare bamboo forest was an essential element conveying the oriental aesthetic of the film, which became the first Chinese-language film to win an Oscar for Best Foreign Language Film, reshaping Western perceptions of Eastern culture and values.

A vast bamboo forest in China can carry both the glint of swords and the soft grace of martial heroes, while also embracing the warmth and cold of life, poetry, and distant dreams. Films like, Like Mist and Rain and Wind, The Legend of the White Snake, and Dwelling Narrowness have drawn even more attention to Anji. The bamboo forest, countryside, and natural charm—within the frame of the screen and beyond the stories—allowed viewers to catch a glimpse of the life they longed for. Thus, from screen to reality, more and more people began to connect with Da Yu Cun in Anji.

Wuhe Village, Yinkeng Village, Yao Family Manor; the Great Bamboo Forest of China, the Tianchi of Jiangnan. Life is like a play, and a play is like life. Strolling through these filming Addresss, meeting a character from a film feels like transcending time and space to converse with them. Perhaps, with a simple turn, you find yourself stepping into a scene, and in that moment, you're part of the story.

## Tips:

If you want to explore Da Yu Cun following the footsteps of movies, you can make the following choices: Great Bamboo Sea of China in Wuhe Village, Tianhuangping Town, is the filming Address of the movie Crouching Tiger, Hidden Dragon and the TV series Like Mist and Rain and Wind; The Jiangnan Tianchi Scenic Area in Tianhuangping Town is the filming Address of the movie Pegasus; Yinkeng Village in Tianhuangping Town is the filming Address of movies such as The Banquet and The Matrimony; The Yao Family manor in Jingcun Village, Tianhuangping Town, is the filming Address of the TV series Growing Pains. In addition to experiencing the film and television culture, taking a Country Walk between villages may bring you unexpected surprises.

# 一池碧蓝
# 天地间的壮丽诗篇

文/朱寅

自打从江南天池回来，我逢人就推荐。

理由有三。

首先是风景绝美。它坐落在海拔近千米的天荒坪顶上，以亚洲最大的天荒坪抽水蓄能电站和中国竹乡山峦翠竹为背景，宛如一颗翠色欲滴的稀世明珠，镶嵌在茫茫竹海之中。水是青蓝的，水面如镜，山风吹过，微波粼粼，宛如迎风抖动的蓝绸；天也碧蓝，小朵棉絮一样的云，倒映在湖面，水天一色，仿佛《千与千寻》中的情境成为现实。我生平头一次见到把雄伟壮观的水利工程和纯朴秀丽的自然风光完美融为一体的地方。

其次是可以避暑。这里海拔将近 1000 米，山下 40°C时，天池只有 30°C，站在池边微风拂过，让人舒爽到想仰天长啸！

再次是适合“飙车”。通往江南天池的盘山公路长达 18 千米，九曲十八弯，盘旋缠绕、蜿蜒曲折，十里山路十里景。坡度陡、转弯急，但很宽敞，适合我这种伪老司机在合法范围内“飙车”过瘾，假装自己是秋名山车神。

如此集山的壮丽与水的柔情于一体的美景，怎能不让人陶醉呢？然而，朋友 A 却十分生气，说我骗人，因为她刚刚刷到了某社交软件的避雷帖，说天池天不蓝水浑浊，更糟的是大池子里居然没水，都快见底了。其实，我和那位博主说的都没错，旅游想要看到美景，还是得提前做点小功课。下面就是我给大家整理的攻略。

Tips

## 怎么能看到完美的江南天池？

1. **最佳游览时间**：江南天池是华东第一座大型抽水蓄能电站。它利用电网晚上多余的电，把山下的水抽上来，灌满山顶的池子。等到白天用电高峰期时放水发电。所以江南天池的水位是动态变化的。知道这个原理，那么大家就不要下午去天池了，尤其是夏天的傍晚，是用电最高峰，为了最大限度地发电，天池里的水都放光了。最好是上午来玩，越早越好。如果住在附近的话，强烈推荐到此看日出。

2. **最佳游览天气**：一定要是大晴天！只有晴空万里，才能看到水天一色的绝美景观。千万避开暴雨或黄梅天刚结束时来参观。众所周知，雨后的河流会变得浑浊。天池每天抽山下的河水溪水。大雨天后，山下的水浑，山顶自然一池黄汤。

3. **其他推荐观赏季节**：冬季山顶积雪很厚，雾凇甚是壮观。春天三四月高山杜鹃盛开，碧蓝的水天配上粉红的花海，非常美。

4. **其他注意事项**：天池海拔高，阳光直射，请做好防晒措施。冬季气温较低，请做好保暖工作。严禁钓鱼、捞鱼、下水！天池平均水深 42 米，最深处 72 米，底部是巨大的发电机，请大家珍爱生命。

5. **额外惊喜**：天池旁有天文台。气象条件好的情况下，可以不用仪器直接观察银河。进入天文台需要在官方公众号提前预约。

✉ 天荒坪镇

# A Pool of Azure Blue,
# a Magnificent Poem of Heaven and Earth

Ever since I returned from Jiangnan Tianchi (Heavenly Pool), I've been recommending it to everyone I meet.

There are three reasons.

First, the scenery is absolutely breathtaking. Located on the top of Tianhuangping, nearly 1,000 meters above sea level, it is set against the backdrop of Asia's largest Tianhuangping pumped-storage power station and the lush bamboo-covered mountains of China's bamboo hometown. It resembles a rare, emerald jewel, nestled in the vast bamboo sea. The water is a deep blue, it's surface like a mirror, with mountain winds stirring gentle ripples, like blue silk fluttering in the breeze. The sky is also a clear blue, with small, cotton-like clouds reflecting on the lake's surface, creating a seamless blend of water and sky, as if the scenes from Spirited Away have come to life. It was the first time in my life I've seen such a majestic water conservancy project perfectly blended with pure, exquisite natural beauty.

Second, it's a great place to escape the summer heat. With an elevation of nearly 1,000 meters, while it's 40°C at the foot of the mountain, the temperature at Tianchi is only 30° C. Standing by the pool, with the breeze brushing against you, it feels so refreshing that you'll be tempted to throw your head back and shout in joy!

Third, it's perfect for "speeding". The 18-kilometer winding mountain road to Jiangnan Tianchi is full of twists and turns, with steep slopes and sharp corners, offering ten miles of scenery in every ten miles. Though the road is narrow and curvy, it's spacious enough for someone like me—a pseudo-speedster—to safely indulge in some "speeding" within legal limitation, pretending to be the champion of Akina Mountain.

Such a magnificent blend of mountains and the gentleness of water—how can anyone not be enchanted by such beauty? However, my friend A was quite upset, claiming I was lying. She had just seen a post on a social media platform warning that Tianchi's sky wasn't blue, the water was murky, and worse still, the big pool was almost empty, with the water level nearly dried up. Actually, neither I nor that blogger were wrong. When it comes to tourism, to truly enjoy the beautiful views, one has to do some research in advance. Below is a guide I've put together for everyone.

## Tips:

How can one see the perfect Jiangnan Tianchi?

**Best time:** It's a pumped storage power station. Water level changes. Don't go in the afternoon, esp. summer evenings when power demand is high. Best in the morning. Recommended to watch the sunrise if nearby.
**Best weather:** Must be sunny for the water-sky scenery. Avoid after rainstorms or plum rain season as the water gets muddy.
**Other seasons:** Winter has thick snow and spectacular rime. Spring (March-April) has rhododendrons. Bluer water with pink flowers is extremely beautiful.
**Precautions:** Due to high altitude, please do sun protection. Keep warm in winter. No fishing, scooping fish or entering the water. Average depth 42m, max 72m with a generator at the bottom.
**Extra:** There's an observatory. Can observe the Milky Way with good **weather.** Need to book on the official account.
**Address:** Tianhuangping Town

不得不承认，现在的城市，遵循着以勒·柯布西耶为代表的现代建筑家的概念，集合住宅的单一化让人们的生活也变得单一。可是脱下高效和冷静的外壳，每个人都只剩下一颗心，这颗心是不尽相同的。于是为了寻找取悦自己的方法，你我他都开始往城市边缘走，走到另一个平行世界里。

那就是乡村。

# 重新粉刷的乡村生活

文 / 温瑶瑶

如今的乡村，早已经和小学作文里回忆的夏天纳凉只能摇蒲扇的样子不同了，砖瓦早就重塑了这片土地。每块土地有自己的主人，在他们的努力下，来到这里可以体会到原本的乡村记忆，也可以感受到野生化的城市生活，或者是异国风情，或者是新潮猎奇，所以形成了民宿村落。所有人都可以在这里找到属于自己的乌托邦。

为了探索这份乡村的新奇，我来到了龙王村。

村落沿河而建，所以相关的记忆也流淌着潺潺的水声。记得去的时候是夏天，顺着河流走，就可以看到许多民宿。有的民宿背山面水，在山水间圈出自己的一方天地；有的建在大石头旁，利用地形的层次错落出几层不同的空间；有的是废弃的水电站重建的，遗留下的电机述说的是忘不了的往事。

乡村早已被重新粉刷，而在其中漫游的我们，也总能找到新的颜色去粉刷我们的生活。

Tips

天荒坪、上墅、山川三个乡镇各有各的不同，但是共同的特点就是悠闲、轻松。各个乡镇也有着属于自己的民宿村落，每个村子都十分有特色。如果在城市里过够了1.25倍速的生活的话，那么你就可以奖励自己一场在大余村的休假。可以根据自己的心情，选一处居住，我想一定能让你满意的。

## 天荒坪

山河村石门民宿村落，具有“石门”特色文化，融入现代文化的新潮与特色；大荷山民宿村落（大溪村），古道、古树、古宅、茶园、梯田、溪流，一片大好“荷”山；银坑金家民宿村落，以“夜”为媒，打造全新“夜未央”生活；五鹤村树景坞民宿村落，层层叠叠的梯田上生长的不只是庄稼，还有丰富的艺术生活。

## 上墅

刘家塘村，天目慢谷，在这里享受蜗牛般的慢节奏生活；龙王村，大片竹海中掩映众多古道，还有造纸文化与民间传说丰富生活；董岭村，紧挨浙北大峡谷，与众多金钱松林立在千米海拔之上。

## 山川

大里村，户外活动与艺术家工作室聚集地，满足每一个不想待在室内的瞬间；船村，井空里大峡谷深处的乌托邦，体会最接近隐居的生活。

# The Repainted Rural Life

I must admit, in today's cities, following the concepts of modern architects like Le Corbusier, the uniformity of collective housing has made people's lives equally monotonous. Yet, when we shed the efficient and calm exterior, all that remains is a heart—each one unique in it's own way. Thus, in search of ways to please ourselves, we all begin to move toward the edges of the city, stepping into a parallel world.

That world is the countryside.

Today's countryside is no longer like the one we remember from childhood essays, where summers were spent merely waving a fan for a breeze. The land has long been reshaped with bricks and tiles. Every plot of land has its owner, and through their efforts, here you can experience the original rural memories, as well as the wild, evolving city life. Whether it's exotic charm or modern curiosity, the result is the creation of quaint villages offering homestays. Here, everyone can find their own utopia.

To explore this new countryside, I visited Longwang Village.

The village is built along a river, so its memories flow with the sound of trickling water. I remember going there in summer, walking along the river, and spotting many homestays. Some are nestled against mountains and face the water, creating their own little haven in the midst of the landscape. Others are built beside large stones, using the uneven terrain to craft several distinct levels of space. Some are reconstructed from abandoned hydropower stations, with the leftover machinery telling tales of the past that are hard to forget.

The countryside has long been repainted, and as we wander through it, we too can always find new colors to repaint our lives.

## Tips:

**Tianhuangping:** Shimen Homestay Hamlet in Shanhe Village, where the traditional "Shimen" culture blends seamlessly with modern trends; Daheshan Homestay Hamlet (Daxi Village), a haven of ancient paths, trees, houses, tea fields, terraced rice paddies, and streams, offering a splendid view of "Lotus (He)" (harmony) Mountain; Yinkeng Jinjia Homestay Hamlet, where nights are celebrated with a new "Night Unending" lifestyle; and Wuhe Village Shujingwu Homestay Hamlet, where terraced fields not only yield crops but also foster a rich artistic life.

**Shangshu:** Liujiatang Village, Tianmu Slow Valley, where you can savor a snail-paced lifestyle; Longwang Village, nestled amidst bamboo forests, ancient trails, and a rich heritage of papermaking culture and folklore; Dongling Village, perched beside the Northern Zhejiang Grand Canyon, standing tall alongside pseudolarix forests at an altitude of over a kilometer.

**Shanchuan:** Dali Village, a hub for outdoor activities and artist studios, catering to every moment you crave the outdoors; Chuan Village, a utopia deep within the Jingkongli Grand Canyon, offering a taste of the closest-to-recluse lifestyle.

# 云上天空

Live In Skyland

# 到云上草原
# 做一朵
# 坠落的云

文/温瑶瑶

去云上草原是需要门槛的——不能恐高。从游客中心坐大巴到索道站，再一路乘坐缆车上到山顶，当缆车跨过两三个山脊后，才终于到达目的地。

踏足云上草原的当天，是一个一望无际的晴天。天空蓝得给人一种不真实的感觉，像一片海。看到滑草场附近的草坪时，一股想要尖叫的情绪直冲我的脑门，太美了，仿佛踏进了《海蒂和爷爷》的电影里。当我爬到山顶，再顺着草地滑下来时，感觉自己像一朵坠落的云。

云上草原坐落在海拔上千米的山上，给人一种“手可摘星辰”的错觉。而在这里，各种高空项目显然是重中之重。不仅有玻璃桥、悬空桥，还有悬崖秋千和悬崖蹦极，窝囊的我当然是没有胆量体验的了，光是走过玻璃桥和悬空桥，我就已经失去了全部的力气。

这一日，失去力气的不仅是我，还有我的手机。

生活在平原的我平日常见的也就是丘陵或者更矮的山包，来到这里真是恨不得一步一张照片。睡前还在回味的我，只记得进入梦乡前的最后一个念头是：今天只体验了高空项目，明天一定要把剩下的都玩个遍才行！

Tips

云上草原，是浙北地区的高山旅游度假区。这里春可赏花，夏可避暑，秋可登山，冬可滑雪，打造了“高山悬崖游乐”“星空滑雪”“野奢酒店群”三大内核板块及民宿、温泉度假等配套项目。高山独特的美域，完全颠覆了人们对江南地理的想象。

云上草原纳入大余村景区后，交通将更加便捷。规划中，有三条纵线串联起大余村各主要景点。

如果选择后山那条新建的“天路索道”行走，从余村出发，20 分钟就可以到达云上草原。

## 温情的项目

云上草原也有温情的游玩项目，比如风之谷、云书房等。这些项目，最适合带着喜欢的人一起走过，拍照“拗造型”。

## 属于孩子的

无动力彩虹滑草、云中部落、绿野迷踪等项目，对孩子们特别友好，最适合亲子家庭游玩。这些项目用“不插电”的游乐方式，打造漫步云端的儿童乐园，让孩子们体验不一样的玩乐时光。

## 玩点刺激的

游玩云上草原首先从悬崖乐园开始。这里的所有项目均为户外极限挑战项目，以索道站为基点，从远至近依次是云海栈桥、悬崖秋千、凌空飞步、水晶廊桥、滑翔伞基地等。不少年轻人专门来这里打卡拍照，毕竟一地就能玩转各种惊险项目，这样的场所不多。

## 想住在这里

建在悬崖上的高端酒店，身处云端之上，让你可俯瞰山间美景；提供管家式服务的城堡酒店，让你享受优雅奢华的好时光；坐落于茫茫草原，抬头即见星空的1168星空天文酒店，让你独享一方天籁，沉醉在深邃星辰之中。

✉ 山川乡山川村

## To Become a Falling Cloud on the Skyland

To travel to the SkyLand, one must first meet a certain requirement: no fear of heights. From the visitor center, take a bus to the cable car station, then ascend to the mountaintop by cable car. After crossing two or three mountain ridges, you finally reach your destination. The day I arrived at the grassland above the clouds, the sky was boundless and clear. The blue was so vivid it almost felt unreal, like an ocean. When I saw the meadow near the grass-skiing area, an overwhelming urge to scream surged within me. It was so beautiful, like stepping into a scene from Heidi. So, when I climbed to the top of the mountain and then slid down the grass, it felt as if I were a cloud falling to the earth.

The Skyland is perched on a mountain over a thousand meters above sea level, giving the illusion that you could "pluck the stars from the sky." Here, various high-altitude activities are clearly the main attractions. Not only are there glass bridges and suspension bridges, but also cliff swings and bungee jumps. As someone who lacks the courage, I certainly didn't try them. Just walking across the glass bridge and suspension bridge was enough to drain all my energy.

That day, it wasn't just my body that lost energy; so did my phone.

Living on the plains, I'm used to seeing only hills or even smaller mounds, so when I arrived here, I couldn't help but take a photo at every step. Just before falling asleep, I could only remember one thought: "Today, I experienced only the high-altitude activities; tomorrow, I must try everything else!"

## Tips:

**Exciting**

Playing starts from the cliff paradise. Projects are extreme challenges. From the cableway station, there are the Cloud Study, Sea of Clouds Trestle Bridge, Cliff Swing, etc. Many young people come to check in and take photos.

**Warmful**

There are warmhearted projects like Cloud Walkway, Glass Walkway, suitable for walking with loved ones and taking photos.

**For kids**

Projects like unpowered rainbow grass skiing are friendly to kids and for parent-child families. They create a cloud-walking paradise for kids to have different fun.

**To stay**

The cliff hotel lets you overlook the scenery. The castle hotel offers luxury. The Star Astronomy Hotel in the grassland lets you enjoy the stars.

**Address:** Shanchuan Village, Shanchuan Township

# 会当凌绝顶<br>一览众山小

文 / 安然

灵溪山像是一个世外桃源，溪流穿行而过、瀑布倾泻而下，还有那峡谷奇石与只能用双脚丈量的崎岖险陡的山路——在过往，上山只能依靠这条山路。许是这里的山谷深处坐落着千年古刹石佛寺，第一次来这里，便有了一场不期然的相遇。

这场相遇，发生在旅程的起点——观音广场。一眼望去，本以为只是一尊巨大的石雕观音像。走近时却发现，在大观音像下面的广场上，是 33 尊石雕菩萨化身像。我从未见过如此多形态的观音菩萨像，一尊一尊细细地看过去，只见不同的观音雕像下面，都有一块牌子，上面写着相应的标注：持莲观音，护佑子孙卓越，品貌皆优；六时观音，护佑六时吉祥，事事如意……我不由得汗如雨下，这观音菩萨的 33 尊化身如同一面面镜子，映照出我们内心的渴望与追求。每一尊化身，不仅仅是美好愿望的象征，更像是遇见我们的每一个自己。

这些愿望，是我们前进的动力，是我们对生活的美好期待。然而，这不也是我们的欲望吗？这些愿望背后，究竟隐藏着怎样的欲望？

我在菩萨的面前，伫立良久。只见她气定神闲，一腿盘坐，一腿屈膝竖起，双手环膝而抱，飘逸的水袖一直垂到坐着的石龛上。她的牌子上写着：财源广进，生意兴隆。我双手合十，虔诚许愿！我不知道，那是我的愿望，还是我的欲望。

继续往前走，还会遇到什么？宛如人生之路，总是有那么多不期然的相遇。

Tips

## 灵溪山风景区

如今上山可以选择走山路，也可以选择坐缆车。只是坐缆车仍须穿过观音广场再走上一小段山路。山上除却石佛寺，还有新修的悬挑碟形玻璃平台，可以观云海、览众山，也可以练练自己的胆量，虽然依然会战战兢兢、瑟瑟发抖。

✉ 山川乡马家弄

# Ascending the Mountain's Crest: It Dwarfs All Peaks Under Our Feet

Lingxi Mountain feels like a hidden paradise. Streams weave through, waterfalls cascade down, and the strange rocks of the canyon, along with the rugged and steep mountain paths that can only be measured by foot—this was the only way to ascend the mountain in the past. Perhaps it's because deep in the valley here sit's the ancient Shifo Temple, a millennia-old site, that my first visit felt like an unexpected encounter.

This encounter took place at the starting point of the journey—Guanyin Square. At first glance, I thought it was simply a massive stone statue of Guanyin. But as I got closer, I discovered that beneath the grand Guanyin statue in the square stood 33 stone statues of Guanyin's incarnations. I had never seen so many different forms of Guanyin. As I carefully observed each one, I noticed that beneath each statue was a plaque with corresponding inscriptions: "Lotus-holding Guanyin, blesses descendants with excellence and beauty"; "Six-time Guanyin, blesses all six times with prosperity and fulfillment" ... I couldn't help but break into a sweat. These 33 incarnations of Guanyin were like mirrors, reflecting our inner desires and pursuit's. Each incarnation is not only a symbol of beautiful wishes but also like an encounter with each of our own selves.

These wishes are our driving force, our beautiful expectations for life. Yet, aren't they also our desires? What desires lie hidden behind these wishes?

I stood in front of one of the statues for a long time. She was calm and composed, one leg crossed in a meditative pose, the other bent and raised. Her hands embraced her knee, and her flowing water sleeves hung down, nearly touching the stone niche she sat upon. The plaque beneath her read: "Wealth flows abundantly, business prospers." I folded my hands in prayer, sincerely making a wish! I didn't know if it was my wish, or if it was my desire.

As I continued on my journey, I wondered what else I might encounter—just like life's path, always full of unexpected meetings.

## Tips:

Lingxi Moutain Scenic Area

Nowadays, you can choose either to go hiking to climb the Lingxi Mountain or to take the cable car. If you take the cable car ,you still need to pass through the Guanyin Square and then take a short walk ofmountain road.

There is also a newly-built glass platform. It offers views of the sea of clouds and surrounding mountains.

**Address:** Majianong, Shanchuan Township

# 去一棵树下顿悟

文/安然

一个中年人写秋天，多少是有些应景的，人生中开过花，热烈过、勇敢过，到了要沉静下来、向内整理的时候，即使还有激情，大概率也会从容许多，包容许多。允许不同，用一种“我不是我”的客观视角看待他人，看待批判。

中年人与秋天的树，有着某种“惺惺相惜”的情分。生命都来到了“无边落木萧萧下”的时节，是不容回避的；但是心中，仍有着某种“我言秋日胜春朝”的不甘和豪情。也许，带着这样复杂的心情，就该去金钱松森林公园，看看那些树，它们如何面对寂寥的深秋，如何用热烈的颜色装点山川，让生命又温柔，又庄严。

然而，事实上，当你站在这里，在一棵棵俊朗挺拔的金钱松面前，它们坦然地随着季节的变幻而变幻着，黄色的松针挂在树上，也落满一地；你分辨不出其生命的浓度和春天里新生的针叶有何区别，你试图寻找的那点共鸣，在无声的蓬勃的生命力下，荡然无存。

从意识上来看，秋天的树和春天的树，没有不同。中年的你与年轻的你，也应该没有不同。

独立寒秋，看万山红遍，层林尽染。我在一棵树的面前，完成了生命中某种“顿悟”。开始拥抱变化，热爱变化，并且全情绽放每一个阶段的生命颜色。

## 中国金钱松森林公园

这里有5万多棵金钱松，每年深秋，一片金黄色。从松针变黄到落叶的时间很短，只有十多天。其时整个山川壮丽热烈，可以驱车直达山上的观景台，也可以从旁边的井空里大峡谷上去领略不同的秋日胜景。当然，冬天的时候，还能看雪景。

我们去的时候，正好碰上一对上海来的中年夫妇，他们将车停在山上，漫步周边，也是不错的选择。山上还有“狗和田野”移动咖啡屋（森林公园门票68元，就包含了一杯咖啡哦），有天幕、桌椅可以暂作休憩。

✉ 山川乡九亩村

## *Epiphany Beneath a Tree*

When a middle-aged person writes about autumn, it often feels like a reflection of the season itself. Having once bloomed, lived passionately, and been brave, at this stage of life, when it is time to calm down and turn inward, even if there is still passion, it is more likely to be composed and accepting. There is a newfound openness to difference, a shift toward an objective perspective that allows one to view others and criticism without attachment. There is a kind of kinship between middle age and the autumn tree, as both have entered the season of "endless leaves falling with the wind," a season that cannot be avoided. Yet in the heart, there remains a certain unyielding and heroic spirit of "I claim autumn as surpassing the spring dawn." Perhaps with such complex emotions, one should visit the Golden Larch Forest Park, to see those trees. How do they face the solitude of late autumn? How do they use vibrant colors to adorn the mountains, making life both gentle and solemn?

In reality, when you stand there, facing the upright and handsome pines, they change serenely with the passing seasons. The yellow pine needles hang from the trees, scattered on the ground below. You cannot tell the difference in the vitality of these needles compared to the fresh ones from spring. The resonance you were searching for disappears under the silent, thriving vitality of life.

From a conscious perspective, the trees of autumn are not different from those of spring. Similarly, the middle-aged you should not be different from the young you.

In the crisp autumn, as I look out at the mountains dyed in crimson, with layers of forest showing vibrant hues, I find myself standing before a tree, experiencing a kind of epiphany. I begin to embrace change, to love change, and to fully bloom in every phase of life's colors.

## Tips:

Golden Larch Forest Park in China

There are more than 50,000 Golden Larch trees here. Every late autumn, the area is blanketed in a sea of golden color. The period from when the pine needles turn yellow to when they fall is very short, lasting only a little over ten days. During that time, the entire landscape is magnificent and vibrant. You can drive directly to the viewing platform on the mountain, or you can climb up from the nearby Jingkongli Grand Canyon to enjoy the different autumn scenery. Of course, in winter, you can also admire the snowscape.

When we went there, we happened to meet a middle-aged couple from Shanghai. They parked their car on the mountain and took a stroll around, which is also a great option. There is also the "Dog and Field" mobile coffee house on the mountain (the entrance ticket to the forest park is 68 yuan, and it includes a cup of coffee). There are tents and tables and chairs where you can take a short rest.
**Address:** Jiumu Village, Shanchuan Township

# 慢慢的时光

文 / 元一

在南屿山的怀抱里，一条曲折蜿蜒的山路静静铺展，仿佛是大自然精心铺设的指引，引领着我一步步深入这秘境之中。清晨，当第一缕阳光尚未揭开夜色的帷幔，属于南屿山的五六条狗便已兴奋地奔跑在山顶的观景平台上，摇摆的尾巴、接二连三的低吠，都传达着它们对探险的渴望。

这是我自山脚村落起攀爬 1.2 千米后看到的景象，宛如一片遗世独立的仙境。时间是初夏的清晨 6 点。站在这里，撞进眼里的是远山含黛，山脊的流畅线条在晨光中若隐若现，仿佛是大自然用最温柔的笔触，勾勒出的一幅淡雅水墨画卷。随着时间的推移，天边黛青色的层云如同巨幕般缓缓拉开，天与地的界限变得模糊，东方的天际渐渐泛起了红晕，日出即将上演。

那一刻，万籁俱寂，只有狗儿喉咙里偶尔发出的呜呜声，以及云海中偶尔传来的风声。随着太阳缓缓升起，金色的光芒穿透云层，洒满整片山峦，云海被染上了一层金黄，远山的轮廓也变得更加清晰，整个世界被唤醒，

用自己的方式说着“你好，早安”。

在这片宁静而广阔的天地间，时间仿佛变得柔软而缓慢，每一刻都值得细细品味。狗儿们的身影在金色的光芒中跳跃，为这份宁静添上了几分生动与活力。而我，则在这片柔软时光中，触摸到了内心的平静与满足。

我很想把此刻的感受写成一些句子，在微信上发给期待南屿山的友人，他说曾在这里享受过一段安静读书的柔软时光。我想告诉他，我踏着他的脚印寻到同一个地方，想触摸和他收获过的一样的柔软，却不想在这样的时光里，生命被连绵的南屿山一寸一寸地延展，减慢，成了无所想的空白，随便滴上一些什么，就成了永恒。

## Tips

南屿山海拔 1038 米，这里山势挺拔，风光旖旎，四季分明，气候温和，雨水充沛，光照充足，多年平均气温为 15.3℃，非常适合休闲度假。南屿山露营基地位于半山腰，海拔约 420 米，从山脚到南屿山露营基地约 2 千米。没有云雾遮挡的天气，可以远眺南屿山顶。

⊠ 天荒坪镇横路村横园里自然村

### 咖啡

隐在竹林里的听瀑咖啡，位于露营基地的途经点。瀑布名为“白水潭”，咖啡是用山泉水制作的，此处适合发呆、打卡。

### 露营

南屿山非常适合户外运动爱好者，露营基地提供专业的露营帐篷，可野炊、烧烤，赏月、观星也十分适合。

### 民宿

南屿山居，是建于竹林中的酒店式帐篷民宿，一共 10 栋，设施完备整洁，十分亲近自然。房间的大露台可以看到日出，看不到日出的时候可观云海。早餐直接送到房间，热水、电、网络、电视一应俱全，可通过一个红色转梯从民宿区经过露营区走到房车区的游泳池。

### 私享房车

房车区、露营区、南屿山居像梯田一样层层错落，房车区在“梯田”的第三层，与游泳池为邻。躺在房车里观日出的特殊体验值得一试。

## *Slowed Time*

In the embrace of Nanyu Mountain, a winding mountain path quietly unfolds, as though it were a carefully laid-out guide from nature itself, leading me step by step into this hidden realm. In the early morning, before the first rays of sunlight have drawn back the curtain of night, five or six dogs belonging to Nan Yu Mountain are already excitedly running on the scenic platform at the summit. Their wagging tails and series of barks all convey their eagerness for adventure. This is the scene I witnessed after climbing 1.2 kilometers from the village at the foot of the mountain, a scene that seemed like a secluded fairyland. The time is 6 a.m. in early summer. Standing here, I am greeted by distant mountains draped in blue, the smooth ridgelines faintly visible in the morning light, like the most delicate brushstrokes of nature, painting a gentle ink wash. As time passes, the dark blue clouds on the horizon gradually part like a giant curtain, blurring the boundary between sky and earth. The eastern horizon slowly tinges with a rosy hue, signaling that the sunrise is about to unfold. In that moment, the world is utterly silent, with only the occasional whine from the dogs and the whisper of the wind in the sea of clouds. As the sun slowly rises, golden light pierces through the clouds, spreading across the mountains, and the sea of clouds is bathed in a golden glow. The outlines of the distant mountains become clearer, and the entire world is awakened, saying

“Hello, good morning” in it's own way.

In this tranquil and vast space, time seems to soften and slow down, with every moment worthy of careful savoring. The dogs leap joyfully in the golden light, adding a touch of liveliness and vitality to the stillness. And I, in this soft moment of time, touch the peace and contentment within my heart.

I long to write this feeling into a few sentences and send them to a friend who is looking forward to Nanyu Mountain. He once told me that he enjoyed a peaceful reading time here. I want to tell him that I've followed in his footsteps to find the same place, to touch the same softness he experienced, but I don’t want the time here to make life stretch out inch by inch, slow down, and become a blank, where I can pour anything in and it becomes eternal.

## Tips:

Nanyu Mountain is 1038 meters high. It has beautiful scenery and a pleasant climate throughout the year. The camping base is located at an altitude of 420 meters and is 2 kilometers away from the foot of the mountain. On clear days, you can see the top of the mountain.

**Address:** Hengyuanli Natural Village, Henglu Village, Tianhuangping Town

**Coffee**
The coffee shop named "Listening to the Waterfall" in the bamboo forest is on the way. The coffee is made with mountain spring water. It is good for relaxing.

**Camping**
It is suitable for outdoor lovers. There are tents available for picnics and barbecues.This is also a good place for moon and star observation.

**Homestay**
Nanyu Mountain Residence in the bamboo forest has 10 buildings. It is clean and close to nature. The terrace offers a wonderful view. Breakfast is delivered. There are various amenities available. You can go to the pool in the RV area via a spiral staircase.

**RV（Recreational Vehicle）**
The RV area is near the pool. It is worth trying to watch the sunrise in the RV.

只有一个人的旅行，才能听得到自己的声音，
它会告诉你，这世界比想象中宽阔。

Only when traveling alone can you hear your own voice.
It will tell you that the world is broader than you imagine.

# 户外山野

Outdoor Wilderness

# 不用去四川，也能
# 骑“熊猫”

文 / 朱寅

小时候天天盼着去四川，因为听说四川人都是骑熊猫上学的，书包里装的都是竹子，因为熊猫饿了不走路！

2024年暑假，闺蜜拉着我来安吉骑“熊猫”，算是满足了二十多年的执念。

熊猫部落探险乐园是附近最大的“显眼包”，2千米外就能看到一条“玉带”一圈圈缠绕在山间。这是一条高空玻璃漂流栈道。

从入园开始，到处是可爱的熊猫元素，被圆滚滚包围的感觉太幸福啦！来得早不用排队，我们直奔“熊猫上山”，骑“熊猫”慢悠悠地直达山顶，不用自己爬山啦。下了“熊猫”，几步路之外就是“竹间漂流”，一条1.2千米长的全透明高架玻璃滑道，从山顶延伸到山脚，720度双环叠加旋转，穿梭于翠绿竹海间，水花四溅，真是清凉又刺激。

接着，我们又坐了一次“熊猫上山”，直达山顶。这次坐“天路飞车”下山，1314米的滑板车道，360度极限弯道，如同秋名山赛道再现。平时在城市里开车不许漂移，来这里总算是过瘾了，享受了一把狂飙的乐趣！

山脚下大多是适合低龄儿童的无动力游乐项目。其中“坑爹过山车”让人好奇，凑近一看，大家哄堂大笑，原来所谓的“坑爹”就是让老爹挥汗如雨骑单车产生动力，推动孩子坐的过山车前进。

Tips

**| 熊猫部落探险乐园游玩指南**

1. 门票不包含山顶两个刺激项目，购买联票更划算。骑“熊猫”免费，不限次数。
2. 山顶的两个刺激项目，儿童必须有家长陪同。玩“竹间漂流”身高必须超过1.2米，不达标不准上船。
3. 不用事先准备防水衣物。“竹间漂流”提供雨衣，全身包得严严实实。

✉ 山川乡

## You Can Ride a "Panda" Without Going to Sichuan

When I was a child, I always dreamed of going to Sichuan because I had heard that people there rode pandas to school and carried bamboo in their backpacks since pandas would refuse to walk if they were hungry!

The summer vacation in 2024, my best friend dragged me to Anji to ride a "panda," finally fulfilling a childhood dream that had lasted for over twenty years.

The Panda Tribe Adventure Park is the biggest attraction nearby, and from two kilometers away, you can spot a "jade belt" winding around the mountains. It's a high-altitude glass floating walkway.

From the moment we entered the park, we were surrounded by adorable panda elements, and I felt completely embraced by their round, fluffy charm! Since we arrived early, there were no lines. We headed straight for the "Panda Ride," and leisurely rode our pandas to the top of the mountain without having to climb at all. Once we got off the pandas, a few steps away was the "Bamboo Drift" , a 1.2-kilometer-long fully transparent glass slide that extends from the mountaintop down to the base. The 720-degree double loop adds a thrilling twist as you zoom through the lush bamboo forest, splashing water everywhere—so refreshing and exhilarating!

Next, we rode the "Panda Ride" up to the mountain again. This time, we took the "Sky Road Racer" down. The 1,314-meter-long skateboard track has extreme 360-degree turns, just like the legendary mountain racing course from the Autumn Mountain. Normally, drifting in the city is a prohibited, but here, I finally got to satisfy my craving for high-speed thrills!

At the foot of the mountain, most of the attractions are low-energy, fun activities suitable for younger children. Among them, the "Dad's Roller Coaster" caught everyone's attention. When we took a closer look, we couldn't stop laughing—it turns out that the "Dad's Roller Coaster" makes fathers pedal a bike to generate power, pushing the children's coaster forward as they ride!

## Tips:

Guide to the Panda Tribe Adventure Park

For two exciting projects on the peak, children must be accompanied by their parents. "Bamboo Drifting" only allows people with a height of over 1.2 meters.

**Address:** Shanchuan Town

根要扎进土地里，和风一起生存，和竹子一起过冬，和鸟儿一起歌颂春天。

The roots should be planted deep in the soil. Live together with the wind, spend the winter alongside the bamboo, and sing praises to spring together with the birds.

文 / 温瑶瑶

# 像一朵行走于山间的云

在余村骑行那天留下的记忆和村庄本来的模样有关。盛夏的样子初现，在没有风的时刻，太阳的照耀下，每一步前行都让人焦躁。沉浸在这种情绪里的我一路上失去了很多欣赏风景的机会，直到同伴呼喊了我一声，让我转头。

原本我一直以为“豁然开朗”是用在从狭窄到宽阔地方的词语，后来我才知道这种理解太狭隘了。这种突然的“开朗”指的不是地理环境，而是心情。在转头的那一刻，我看到的是连片的荷塘，荷叶已经翠绿而且展开，其中还有几朵盛开的粉色荷花。池塘的边上围着一条步道，接着是几步一棵的大树，然后是潺潺的小溪，完美得像小时候听到的童话故事里描写的那样。随后的路线和记忆十分模糊，但是这一幕却始终像摁下快门的一瞬间那样，在我的记忆

里留下“咔嚓”的声音。

我只知道，我爱上了骑行。

也许是冥冥中的安排，在某一日随性的阅读中，猛然读到了“空阔的大地在历史上颇受冷落，倘若要去爱它，你必须像卡瑟那样相信，美有时是连续空间的一种功能。你必须相信，这样的疆域自有其延展性”。这段话冲击着我的记忆，于是这次我决定去天目山上骑行。

相信我，对于刚刚涉猎骑行的人来说，这并不是件容易的事。上山不容易，骑行十分吃力，遇到略大的坡度需要下车推行；下山更不容易，时不时出现的弯道和下坡让刹车系统显得螳臂当车。但是这是件十分美好的事情，虽是骑到一个不知名的小山坡上，却能窥见在平原上无法看到的景色。山上的风掠过，带来的是背后山间树林里的味道和气息，面前是一望无际的旷野。虽然只是100多米高的小山坡，但是彼时，我认为自己站在了喜马拉雅的山巅，成为 the king of the world。

那一刻，我的多巴胺分泌到了极致。

## Tips

骑行可以是自己一个人的故事，也可以是一群人的故事。如果想找到组织，在大余村的“青来集”内有个OKKA骑行社，可以在里面找到喜欢骑行的同好哦。

### 骑行路线

入门：乡村游览路线，可以慢慢悠悠地骑，边骑边观赏景色，平均骑行时间在一个小时上下。

1. 余村—银坑村
2. 刘家塘—蜗牛谷

进阶：沿途经过较大的景区，一圈大概50千米，海拔爬升大概600米。

船村—云上草原—余村

高阶：难度较大，适合具有挑战意图的“玩家”。

余村—江南天池

### 骑行装备

1. 车：在乡村或者平坦的路上骑行，可以选择任意车辆，甚至是路边的公共自行车；如果要去山地骑行，则需要选择相应的可以变速的山地车。

2. 护具：护具包括骑行服、骑行头盔、骑行手套、太阳眼镜等，选择重点是轻盈、透气、防风，在骑行的过程中如果遇到意外情况可以尽量保护自己。

3. 其余用品：车灯，车头、车尾都装上一个，选择续航力强、防水的；码表或者手表等记录器，记录自己路上的骑行数据；耳机，看个人需要，有时候适当听音乐可以帮助更好地前行。

## *Walking in the Mountains Like a Cloud*

The memories I have of cycling in Yucun Village are tied to the village's original charm. The early signs of summer were just beginning to show. On days with no breeze, the sun's heat made every step feel more agitating. Immersed in this restless mood, I missed many opportunities to appreciate the scenery until one of my companions called out to me, urging me to turn around.

I always thought the phrase "a sudden clarity or moment of enlightenment (huo ran kai lang)" applied only to physical spaces, like moving from a narrow area to a wide-open one. But I later realized my interpretation was too narrow. This sudden clarity isn't about geography—it's about mood. The moment I turned around, I saw an expansive lotus pond. The lotus leaves were a vibrant green, spread wide, and a few pink blossoms were in full bloom. Around the pond was a walking path, followed by a series of trees spaced evenly apart, and beyond them, a babbling creek. It was like something out of the fairy tales I'd heard as a child. The rest of the route and memories are hazy, but that scene remains etched in my mind, as vivid as the click of a camera shutter.

I knew then, I had fallen in love with cycling.

Maybe it was fate, or perhaps a random reading one day, but I suddenly came across a line that struck a chord: "The vast earth has long been neglected in history, and if you are to love it, you must believe, as Cassir said, that beauty is sometimes a function of continuous space. You must believe that such territories have their own expansiveness." This passage left a deep impact on me, and so, this time, I decided to cycle up Mount Tianmu.

Believe me, for someone just starting out with cycling, this is no easy feat. Going uphill is tough, every pedal feels like a challenge, and when the slope steepens, you have to get off and push the bike. Going downhill isn't much easier—curves and descents make the braking system feel like it's fighting a losing battle. But it's a wonderful experience. Even on an unknown little hill, I could see a view that's impossible to find on the flat plains. The wind on the mountain carries the scent of the woods behind me, and ahead, the endless wilderness stretches out. Though it was only a 100-meter high hill, at that moment, I felt like I stood atop the Himalayas, the king of the world.

At that moment, my dopamine levels surged to the highest point.

## Tips:

Solo or group cycling? Join OKKA Cycling Club in  for like-minded enthusiasts.

Routes:

**Beginner:** Leisurely rural routes, 1-hour ride. (Yuncun Village -

Yinkeng Village, Liujiatang–Snail Valley)
**Intermediate:** Scenic 50km routes, 600m elevation. (The Skyland–Yuncun Village)
**Advanced:** Challenging routes. (Yuncun Village–Jiangnan Tianchi)
Equipment:
**Bicycle:** Any for rural/flat rides; mountain bike for mountains.
Protective gear: Lightweight, breathable, windproof clothing, helmets, gloves, sunglasses.
**Essentials:** Strong, waterproof front/rear lights; cyclocomputer/watch; headphones (optional).

## Cycling Equipment

1.Bicycle: When cycling in the countryside or on flat roads, you can choose any vehicle, even the public bicycles by the roadside. If you are going to cycle in the mountains, you need to choose a mountain bike with variable speed accordingly.
2. Protective Gear: Protective gear includes cycling clothes, cycling helmets, cycling gloves, sunglasses, etc. The key points for selection are lightness, breathability and wind resistance. In case of unexpected situations during cycling, it can protect yourself as much as possible.
3. Other Supplies: Lights for the bicycle, install one at the front and one at the rear of the bicycle. Choose those with strong battery life and waterproof function. Record devices such as a cycling computer or a watch to record the cycling data on the road. Headphones are optional according to personal needs. Sometimes listening to music appropriately can help you move forward better.

# 去吧！去走不被定义的 Whatever Walk

文 / 刘林

如果在这几年新兴的词语中，让我选一个最喜欢的，那大概就是 City Walk，城市漫步。

漫步，是一个很值得推敲的词。“漫”字由水的溢出而引申出自在、无拘无束的意义。水会漫出，必是因为有容器，是突破了某种限制。漫步，便意味着，可以少一些条条框框，更为自由地去看这个地方。文化、历史、建筑、美食往往以一种不经意的方式，与人邂逅。

City Walk 这个词本身就是源自 London Walks（伦敦漫步）。于是，我也知道了，Walk 是不被框定的。

大余村可以有 Country Walk。大余村的村落布局并非千篇一律，每个角落都散发着各自独特的韵味与特色。有的村落依山傍水，展现出温婉灵动的江南水乡风情；有的则坐落于连绵起伏的山丘之上，错落有致的石板路、古朴的民居与远处的青山相映成趣，构成了一幅幅动人的田园诗画。

可以有 Hill Walk。这里的山峦虽不险峻，却也别有一番风味。沿着蜿蜒的山道拾级而上，两旁是郁郁葱葱的树木和偶尔传来的鸟鸣声，让人瞬间忘却尘世的烦恼。

可以有 Forest Walk。沿着小路穿入一片片茂密的竹林、松林，它们或在夏季挺拔而翠绿，或在秋日金黄璀璨，踏在柔软而富有弹性的树叶上，能让心灵获得前所未有的放松与净化。

大余村，可以是 Whatever walk。

## Tips

**请接收来自大余村的徒步指南！**

### ♥ 山川漫步指南

长度：12千米　步行时长：4小时　最高海拔：925米

* 船村因其村庄轮廓形似小船而得名，四面青山环抱，溪流穿村而过，闲暇时在村中漫步也是不错的选择。

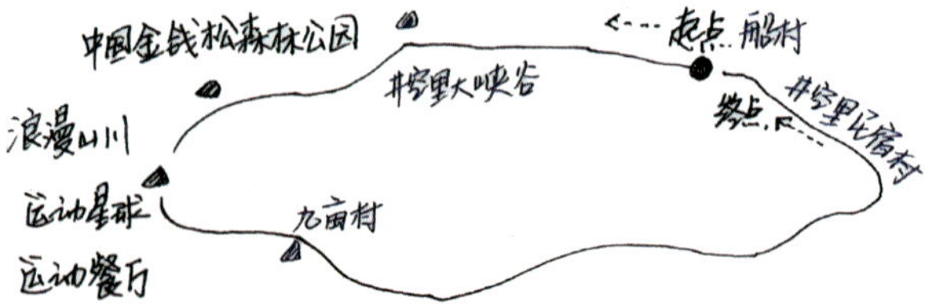


### ♥ 天荒坪漫步指南

长度：14千米　步行时长：4小时　最高海拔：1050米

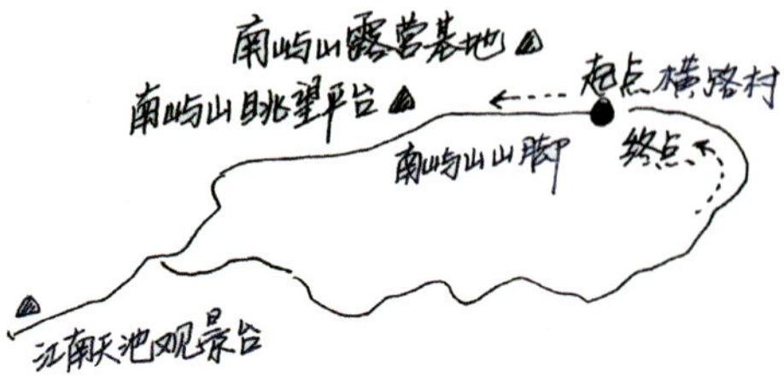


* 从南屿山山脚至南屿山眺望平台约 1.2 千米，可先驱车前往南屿山眺望平台，后开展前往更高海拔处和江南天池的徒步活动，沿途道路较原始，徒步强度较高。

### ♥ 上墅漫步指南

* 起点处有一座安吉古道文化博物馆。

长度：11千米　步行时长：2小时　最高海拔：909米

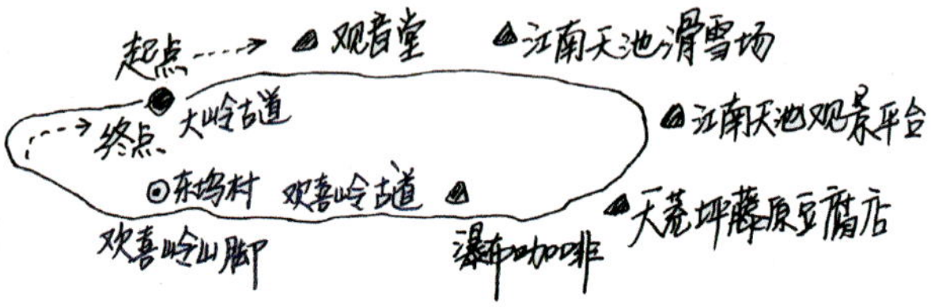

# *Go! Take the Walk that's Not Defined —The Whatever Walk*

If I had to pick my favorite newly emerging term in recent years, it would probably be "City Walk." "Walk" is a word that's worth contemplating.

The Chinese character "man", derived from the overflowing of water, suggests a sense of freedom, boundlessness. Water overflows because it has a container; it breaks a certain limit. Similarly, "man bu" or "strolling," means being free from constraints, allowing oneself to explore a place more freely. Culture, history, architecture, and food often encounter us in the most unintentional ways.

The term "City Walk" originates from "London Walks". So, I learned that a "walk" is not something that is confined.

In Da Yu Cun, you may experience a "Country Walk". The village layout isn't uniform; each corner has it's own unique charm and character. Some areas nestle by rivers and mountains, displaying the gentle beauty of a Jiangnan water town, while others sit atop rolling hills, where cobbled paths, ancient homes, and distant green mountains form a picturesque rural scene.

You may also encounter a "Hill Walk": The hills here may not be steep, but they have their own distinctive appeal. Climbing the winding mountain paths, surrounded by lush trees and the occasional bird song, you'll instantly forget the troubles of the world.

There could even be a "Forest Walk," where you wander along narrow paths through dense bamboo and pine forests. In summer, the trees stand tall and vibrant green, while in autumn, they shimmer with golden hues. Walking on the soft, springy leaves, you'll feel a relaxation and purification of the soul like never before.

Da Yu Cun may offer you a "Whatever Walk".

## Tips:

Receive your guide to walking in !

**♥ Shanchuan Walk Guide**

Chuancun Village got it's name because it's village outline is shaped like a small boat. Surrounded by green mountains on all sides, a stream runs through the village. Taking a stroll in the village during one's leisure time is also a great option.

**Length:** 12km **Walking duration:** 4h **Highest altitude:** 925m

**♥ Tianhuangping Walk Guide**

It is about 1.2 kilometers from the foot of Nanyu Mountain to the viewing platform of Nanyu Mountain. You can first drive to the viewing platform of Nanyu Mountain, and then start the hiking activities to higher altitudes and the Jiangnan Tianchi. The roads along the way are relatively primitive, and the hiking intensity is high.

**Length:** 14km **Walking duration:** 4h **Highest altitude:** 1050m

**♥ Shangshu Walk Guide**

There is an Anji Ancient Road Culture Museum at the starting point.

**Length:** 11km **Walking duration:** 2h **Highest altitude:** 909m

# 爱跑山
# 不爱运动

文/温瑶瑶

“能够来参加跑山，其实也是一种幸运。根据每个地区跑山比赛的要求，有重大疾病或先天疾病的患者以及其他不适宜运动的人都不能参加跑山，这代表着你的身体如今还有着坚不可摧的健康。”朋友为了让我运动，正在无所不用其极地瞎说。

“但是跑完这段可就不一定了。”我没有接茬，却在心里恶狠狠地骂了一句。讨厌自律和运动是我的人生标签，我只是在贯彻自己的人设。

因为旅游，朋友见这里生态如此之好，连哄带骗把我带到了南屿山下。还没等我骂完，朋友便拉着我跑了起来。

突如其来的慢跑让我呼吸变得急促，加上满身的怨气，还没到 10 分钟，我就仿佛浑身灌了铅。正想放弃的时候，身边突然出现了一只毛茸茸的东西，原来是附近民宿的老板带着自家的“毛孩子”也在跑山。如此一来，我便有了动力。这之后我就发现，跑山原来也是有可取之处的。

那时虽然是夏天，但是我们来得早，还属于清晨，太阳还不是很毒，所以可以看见平常白天躲起来的生物。更幸运的是，因为前一天下了雨，还出现了许多新东西，比如路边树下刚冒出来的小菌菇头，还开着伞盖；比如飞流直下十几尺的瀑布，在丛林的掩映下哗啦啦地呼唤着我们，我们却因为附近石头上长着许多青苔不敢靠近；比如各种各样颜色的野花，在路边，在半山腰，在崖壁上。

原本我计划了一个小时的运动时间，朋友还嗤之以鼻，到后面朋友几次想返程，却只能看到我因为发现新事物而兴奋蹿出去的背影。

人生啊，果然还是要体验过后才知道是什么滋味。事已至此我只能说，我爱跑山，但是我还是不爱运动。

Tips

跑山又称为越野跑，通常指在山区或野外进行的徒步、越野、攀登等活动。跑山也分业余的和专业的，业余的指自己日常的活动，没有什么限制；专业的话可以选择去参加比赛。每年大余村附近几个乡镇都有相关的比赛，路程从 5 到 21 千米不等，欢迎有意愿的小伙伴们踊跃参与。

## 装备

跑山的时候最好轻装上阵，但是也可以根据自己的习惯带一些装备。

1. 防水冲锋衣裤、墨镜、运动鞋等。穿一双抓地力强的运动鞋，虽然不能让我们在山上如履平地，但是却能最大程度上让路更好走。另外，墨镜遮挡阳光，冲锋衣裤缓解山脚和山顶温差大的问题，这些装备都能最大程度地保护我们的安全。
2. 水和食物。跑山时间通常较长，体力消耗大，可以随身携带软水壶和饼干等主食。

## 路线

1. 龙王山路线（简单版）：龙王古道文化展示馆—眼前山—曹家坞—大溪上培—龙王古道文化展示馆。
2. 天荒坪镇路线：南屿山露营基地—江南天池。

# I Love Mountain Running, But Not Exercise

"Being able to join this mountain run is actually a kind of luck. According to the requirements for mountain running in different regions, people with major illnesses, congenital conditions, or other health issues are not allowed to participate. That means your body is still strong and healthy, indestructible." My friend, in an effort to get me to exercise, was using every trick in the book, spouting nonsense.

"But once we finish this part, who knows?" I didn't respond, but inside I cursed. I've always had the label of disliking discipline and exercise—it's just who I am, after all.

We were here because of a trip, and seeing how pristine the local ecology was, my friend tricked and persuaded me to come to the foot of Nanyu Mountain. Before I could even finish cursing, my friend grabbed my hand and started jogging.

The sudden burst of jogging left me panting, and with all the frustration building up, I felt like I was dragging lead weights. Just under 10 minutes in, I was ready to quit, when out of nowhere, a fluffy creature appeared beside me. It was the owner of a nearby guesthouse, running up the mountain with his "fur baby" .That gave me a boost of energy. I soon realized there was more to mountain running than I had expected.

Although it was summer, we had arrived early enough for it to still be morning, and the sun wasn't too harsh yet. This gave us a chance to see creatures usually hidden during the day. Even luckier, because it had rained the day before, there were so many new sights to see: little mushrooms just sprouting at the base of the trees, their caps open like tiny umbrellas; a waterfall cascading down a cliff, hidden by the jungle, calling to us with it's roaring sound—but we couldn't get too close because of the moss on the rocks nearby; wildflowers in all sorts of colors lining the roadside, scattered on the hillsides and even growing out of the cliff walls.

I had planned to only exercise for an hour, but my friend scoffed at me. As time passed, though, when my friend wanted to turn back, all he could see was my excited figure darting ahead, captivated by yet another new discovery.

Life, it turns out, is all about experiencing things to know their true flavor. At this point, all I can say is, I love mountain running, but I still don't love exercise.

## Tips:

Mountain running, also known as trail running, usually refers to activities such as hiking, cross-country running, and climbing carried out in mountainous areas or the wild. Mountain running can be divided into amateur and professional categories. Amateur mountain running refers to one's daily activities without many restrictions. For professionals, they can choose to participate in competitions. Every year, there are relevant competitions in several townships near Dayu Village, with the distances ranging from 5 to 21 kilometers. We welcome interested friends to actively participate.

**Equipment :**

When going mountain running, it's best to travel light, but you can also bring some equipment according to your own habit's.

1.Waterproof jackets and pants, sunglasses, sports shoes, etc. These pieces of equipment can protect our safety to the greatest extent.

2.Water and food. Mountain running usually takes a long time and consumes a lot of physical strength. You can carry a soft water bottle and staple foods like biscuits with you.

**Routes:**

**Longwang Mountain Route (Easy Version):** Longwang Ancient Path Culture Exhibition Hall–Yanqian Mountain–Caojiawu–Daxishangpei–Longwang Ancient Path Culture Exhibition Hall.

**Tianhuangping Town:** Nanyu Mountain Camping Base–Jiangnan Tianchi.

# 在喧哗与宁静之间一键切换

文 / 刘林

第一次，来到山川乡的大里村，是一个黄昏，一个热闹的黄昏。

时值黄昏，大里村披上了一层金色的外衣。沿着湖边的游步道行走，湖面闪烁着点点金光，与不远处的青山相互映衬。

咖啡屋内，人人手捧一杯香浓的咖啡，透过落地窗远眺那山、那水、那云，和身旁的友人闲聊打趣；游人在教练的指导下，在湖面上自由划桨，感受水上运动的乐趣与刺激；烧烤的气氛已经开始烘托起来，就等着太阳落山，与亲朋好友围炉而坐，共享一顿丰盛的烧烤盛宴。这里热闹，却并不吵闹，更像是人间烟火的具象化。置身其中，自己也成了烟火的一份子。

再次来到大里村，是一个午后，一个安静的午后。阳光透过轻纱般的云层，洒落在这片被翠绿竹林温柔拥抱的净土上，营造出一种难以言喻的和谐氛围。四周，除了偶尔传来的竹叶摩挲声和湖面的潺潺水声，几乎听不到其他任何嘈杂声。

我与友人寻找到一处竹荫下的露营椅

坐下，耳边是轻柔的风声与鸟鸣，心中是一片空明与宁静。明明是两个人的场景，却谁也不想说话，各自沉浸在眼前的静谧氛围之中，一切纷扰和烦恼都随风而去。

任谁也想不到写下上面几句“岁月静好”漂亮话的我，在进入这里之前，被太阳暴晒得像一条狂躁的狗。大概，拥有一片竹林小天地，就是躺平的秘诀吧。

## Tips

### 山川乡有哪些地方，可以一键切换喧哗与宁静？

#### 1. 云下湖畔自然乡村艺术馆 咖啡·露营·桨板

云下湖畔自然乡村艺术馆依湖而建，面朝青山碧湖，是一个集咖啡、露营、桨板、美术馆、图书馆于一体的艺术天堂。因此，想要在这样一个地方去寻一份清静再简单不过了，或是在图书馆内静静翻阅一本书，或是拿着咖啡在山后竹林里漫步，都是十分惬意的选择。

✉ 山川乡大里村罗仲自然村

#### 2.In·竹野躺平基地

In · 竹野躺平基地是由一个普通旧水库（水塘）改造而来的户外休闲空间。躺平的方式有许多种，欢快一些也未尝不可，或是畅游水上桨板，或是等到夜幕降临在酒吧内喝上一杯。这里的餐饮主打一个差异化，以西餐为主。试想一下，在竹林里喝鸡尾酒、吃西餐，是何种奇妙的体验。

✉ 山川乡大里村桃坑水库

## *Seamlessly Switch Between Bustle and Tranquility*

The first time I visited Dali Village in Shanchuan Township, it was a bustling twilight.

As the sun began to set, Dali Village was draped in a golden glow. Strolling along the lakeside promenade, the surface of the water sparkled with golden specks, reflecting the nearby green hills.

Inside the cafe, everyone cradled a cup of rich, fragrant coffee, gazing out through the floor-to-ceiling windows at the mountains, the water, the clouds, and chatting casually with friends. Tourists, under the guidance of their instructors, were paddling freely on the lake, enjoying the fun and excitement of water sports. The scent of barbecuing food was starting to fill the air, just waiting for the sun to dip below the horizon, when friends and family would gather around the grill to share a hearty feast. It was lively here, but not noisy—more like a tangible manifestation of the simple joys of life. Surrounded by this atmosphere, I felt myself being woven into the living tapestry of this world.

When I returned to Dali Village again, it was an afternoon—a peaceful afternoon. The sunlight filtered through the gossamer clouds, casting a gentle glow over the land, which was tenderly embraced by lush green bamboo forests, creating an indescribable

sense of harmony. Surrounding us, the only sounds were the occasional rustling of bamboo leaves and the gentle murmur of the lake, with no other noise in sight.

My friend and I found a pair of camping chairs beneath the shade of the bamboo, where the soft breeze and the birds' songs filled our ears. In that moment, our minds were clear, and peace . Though we were two, neither of us felt the need to speak—each of us immersed in the quiet atmosphere, letting go of all the noise and worries that had once weighed us down.

No one would believe that the person who wrote the beautiful words above about "peaceful times" was, just moments before arriving here, scorched by the sun like a frantic dog. I suppose, having your own little bamboo grove is the secret of both lying flat and finding peace.

## Tips:

What are the places in Shanchuan Township where one can enjoy tranquility?

**1. Cloudy Lake Natural Countryside Art Gallery**
**Coffee, Camping, Paddleboarding**

Built alongside the lake, facing green mountains and a clear lake, Cloudy Lake is an artistic paradise that integrates coffee, camping, paddleboarding, an art gallery, and a library. Therefore, finding a quiet spot in such a place is quite simple—whether it's quietly reading a book in the library or strolling through the bamboo grove behind the mountain with a coffee in hand, both are delightful choices.

**Address:** Luozhong Natural Village, Dali Village, Shanchuan Township

**2. In•Bamboo Wilderness Chill-Out Base**

The In•Bamboo Wilderness Chill-Out Base is an outdoor leisure space transformed from an ordinary old reservoir (pond). There are many ways to chill out, and having fun is also an option—whether it's enjoying paddleboarding on the water or having a drink at the bar as night falls. The dining here focuses on uniqueness, mainly offering Western cuisine. Imagine what a peculiar experience it would be to sip cocktails and enjoy Western food in the bamboo grove.

**Address:** Taokeng Reservoir, Dali Village, Shanchuan Township

# 青年在村

Youth in the Village

带着血脉的牵绊和成长的记忆，大余村的原乡青年对故土有着深深眷恋。
春日里万物复苏的田野，夏日里蝉鸣四起的树林，
秋日里金黄的稻田，冬日里皑皑的白雪，
这些景象如同烙印一般，刻在他们心间，成为永恒不变的乡愁。
乡愁是一成不变的底色，
新乡村则成为他们释放豪迈激情的旷野乐园。

# 原乡人<br>似孩童，总依恋

# The Natives: Childlike Attachment Forever

Bound by the ties of blood and memories of growth, the native youth of Da Yu Cun carry a deep love for their homeland.

In spring, the fields come to life, in summer, the trees buzz with the chirping of cicadas, in autumn, the rice paddies glow with golden hues, and in winter, the snow blankets the earth in pure white.

These scenes are like imprints, etched into their hearts, becoming an everlasting nostalgia.

Nostalgia is the unchanging backdrop,

While the new countryside has become their boundless playground, where they can unleash their youthful vigor.

# / 回家<br>用平常心做不平凡的事 /

文 / 温瑶瑶

“他们的生命淌进我的生命，而我的生命，亦是他们的支流。其中自然有不同，但在很多方面却比我原以为的，要相似得多。”

这是俞佳慧生活的真实写照。在上一辈潜移默化的影响下，出于对自然的尊重和喜爱，促使她在一次次寻找工作的旅途中选择了终将会通往与余农场的那个拐点。这是缘分，也是命运。也许是许多青年回乡的榜样使然，在全家人的支持下，俞佳慧回到了家乡，开启了与余农场的故事。

创业不易，贵在有伴同行。一个伴是自己的父亲宝哥，他为孩子的事业提供了全心全意的技术支持；一个伴是另一位全球合伙人张赟，见多识广的他在与余生态农场的定位、项目宣传、推广等方面都为俞佳慧提供了不小的助益。俞佳慧也在这个过程中像海绵一样不断地吸收知识，来丰富自己和农场。创办与余农场的初心和愿景，是从自身和身边的朋友出发，试图在快节奏却又有些茫然的生活中为年轻人打造休憩身心的场所。年轻人的朋

**关键词**
**与余农场主理人　中国共产主义青年团第十九次全国代表大会代表**

友圈涵盖亲子、情侣、朋友，与余农场以可爱动物为媒介，通过各种主题活动，如围炉煮茶，为来到这里的人们提供原生态的生活体验。

如今，在俞佳慧的努力下，与余农场的故事也越来越精彩。她每天都忙得脚不沾地，但十分开心。余村也正是因为有了这些全球合伙人，举目皆新。

## / Going Home: Doing Extraordinary Things with a Ordinary Heart /

"Their lives flow into mine, and my life is, in turn, a tributary of theirs. There are certainly differences, but in many ways, we are far more alike than I ever imagined." This is a true reflection of Yu Jiahui's life.

Under the subtle influence of the previous generation, driven by her respect and love for nature, Yu Jiahui, during her many job-searching journeys, chose the path that would ultimately lead her to a turning point at Yuyu Farm. It was fate, and it was destiny. Perhaps inspired by the examples of many young people returning to their hometowns, with the full support of her family, Yu Jiahui returned to her roots and began her story with Yuyu Farm.

Entrepreneurship is not easy, but the key is having companions along the way. One companion is her father, Bao Ge, who wholeheartedly supports his child's venture with technical expertise. Another companion is her global partner, Zhang Yun, a well-traveled and knowledgeable individual who has greatly helped Yu Jiahui with positioning Yuyu Farm, project promotion, and publicity. Throughout this journey, Yu Jiahui has absorbed knowledge like a sponge, enriching both herself and the farm. The original vision for founding Yuyu Farm was to create a retreat space for young people in the fast-paced, somewhat uncertain world, starting with her own experience and the needs of her friends. The young people's social circle, including parents, couples, and friends, connects with Yuyu Farm through adorable animals and various themed activities, such as tea boiling around the fire, providing an authentic, natural living experience for those who visit.

Today, thanks to Yu Jiahui's efforts, the story of Yuyu Farm grows ever more wonderful. She is busy from dawn to dusk, but is truly happy. Yucun Village is also changing for the better, thanks to these global partners, with fresh energy in every corner.

**Keywords:**
Owner of Yuyu Farm, Delegate to the 19th National Congress of the Communist Youth League of China

# / 音乐、酒与伙伴 /

文 / 元一

傍晚在余村散步，往乡音小馆那条路走过去，而后到余村大草坪，那里有青年图书馆和国漫咖啡馆。乡音小馆就像这条 Country Walk 路线上的灯塔——不仅因为建筑高度，还因为它明亮、温暖的灯光。和黄斌、陈镇宇的聊天就是在一扇落地玻璃窗旁的桌子边开始的。

做广告策划的黄斌与做设计的陈镇宇，是因为余村的垃圾站而联系在一起的，这个垃圾站就是乡音小馆的前身。从垃圾站到乡音小馆，黄斌和陈镇宇只用了 48 天就完成这个空间的蝶变。

乡音小馆的空间主题是音乐和酒。黄斌说余村的咖啡店很多且各有特色，加上乡村夜生活几乎都是烧烤的主场，他们想做点不一样的。和一些安吉的音乐人聊过以后，小酒馆的思路就有了雏形，两个伙伴根据自己的想法和感觉开始改造垃圾站。陈镇宇保留了原先垃圾站的院墙，并对这个空间做了重塑，就有了现在余村夜晚里这一墙透明的暖暖灯光。

小酒馆不仅是游客夜晚放松的地方，也是黄斌、陈镇宇和朋友们相聚尽欢的自在空间。晚上10点半以后，酒馆的舞台主场就交给了客人和音乐老师，音乐老师也是小酒馆的合伙人。余村有全球青年合伙人计划，小酒馆的运营理念与此同出一辙。除了酒馆的经营，黄斌与合伙人还针对小朋友和在安吉的年轻人，做了30多期音乐公益活动以及流浪课堂。

黄斌和陈镇宇都很爱笑。二人笑称过往的工作几乎和乡村振兴不搭边，但因为这个小酒馆，他们成了美丽乡村建设中一个小小的细胞，小而美好。

**关键词**

**山系森活主理人　乡音小馆主理人　户外爱好者**

## / Music, Wine, and Friends /

In the evening, I take a walk in Yucun Village, heading down the road toward Xiangyin Tavern, then on the Yucun Village Lawn, where you'll find the Youth Library and Guoji Cafe. Xiangyin Tavern is like a lighthouse along this Country Walk route—not just because of it's height, but because of it's bright, warm lights. My conversation with Huang Bin and Chen Zhenyu began at a table next to a large glass window.

Huang Bin, an advertising planner, and Chen Zhenyu, a designer, were brought together by the village's former garbage station, which later transformed into Xiangyin Tavern. From garbage station to tavern, Huang Bin and Chen Zhenyu completed this space's metamorphosis in just 48 days.

The theme of Xiangyin Tavern is music and wine. Huang Bin mentioned that while there are many coffee shops in Yucun Village, each with it's own unique charm, the local nightlife is mostly dominated by barbecue spots, so they wanted to do something different. After chatting with a few musicians from Anji, the concept for the small tavern began to take shape. The two partners started transforming the old garbage station based on their ideas and instincts. Chen Zhenyu kept the original walls of the garbage station and reimagined the space, creating the warm, transparent glow that now lights up the village at night.

The small tavern serves not only as a place for visitors to unwind in the evening, but also as a casual space for Huang Bin, Chen Zhenyu, and their friends to gather and enjoy. After 10:30 pm, the tavern's stage is handed over to the guests and the music teacher, who is also a partner in the tavern. Yucun Village runs a global youth partnership program, and the tavern's operational philosophy aligns with this initiative. In addition to running the tavern, Huang Bin and his partners have organized over 30 music charity events and wandering classrooms for children and young people in Anji.

Huang Bin and Chen Zhenyu both love to laugh. They jokingly say that their past work had little to do with rural revitalization, but because of this little tavern, they've become small yet meaningful cells in the construction of a beautiful countryside.

**Keywords:**

Owner of Mountain Series Forest Life, Owner of Xiangyin Tavern, Outdoor Enthusiast

# / 斜杠青年奋斗史 /

文 / 元一

顶着一个十分洋气的名字，在乡村稳重地做着很有年轻活力的事——她是查李苏，她是天荒坪镇大溪村 90 后村党总支书记。

“做村书记，就像是给我的人生打开了一个新世界。”在言语简洁、雷厉风行的查李苏的职业规划中，原本没有关于“村书记”这个角色设定的想象。从军两年，退伍后返回大学，在校创业开民宿，再到上市公司任职，一转身又踏进象牙塔教书育人。她原以为会顶着“老师”的光环一路走下去。然而乡村振兴的迭代升级呼唤着年轻的力量，查李苏就这样迎着家乡的期待，以“乡村振兴新青年”的身份回村成为一名“村官”，从酷帅的“查老师”变成了“小查书记”。

当工作环境变换为自己的家乡，工作面对的人群是自己的左邻右舍，年轻的小查书记还是有点“水土不服”。不过年轻的魅力和感染力就在于目标清晰、一往无前。村干部“老中青”的年龄构成是查李苏带领大溪村文旅转型升级的底气，将事情摆在台面上和大家一起商量是她为人做事的坦诚，带着年轻干部仔细谋划、踏实执行、运营乡村发展则让我们看到如今大溪村生气勃勃的模样。

“今年我们村班子在全县‘实干争先擂台赛’上拿到了最高荣誉，已经签约的业态落地大半；明年乡村里的第一家‘星巴克’将会出现在大溪村，这会成为一个现象级事件。”“乡村永远是都市的温厚的承载力量，是未来最大的奢侈品。我希望它既保留乡愁的温情，又焕发年轻的活力。”

如果不是看着面前的人，很难想象这是才走马上任一年的“村书记”。“做村干部要有奉献精神，没有情怀是做不了的。”

**关键词**
**90 后村党总支书记　乡村振兴新青年　运动达人**

老成持重的另一面是小查书记的自我留白。1 周 2 天的运动时间、1 年 7 天的休假安排、一些碎片空当的阅读静心，这是查李苏的“个人”时光，是她“5+2”“白 + 黑”工作状态里的轻松韵律。

当被问及自己的名字时，她笑得俏皮：“我和金庸大师是本家，李是母亲的姓，至于‘苏’嘛，就得去找父母亲大人找答案啦！”

## / The Struggles of a Slasher /

With a rather fashionable name, she is steadily pursuing youthful and vibrant endeavors in the countryside—she is Zha Lisu, the post-90s Party Secretary of Daxi Village in Tianhuangping Town.

"Becoming the village party secretary was like opening a new world in my life." In the straightforward and decisive career plan of Zha Lisu, there was no room for the role of "village party secretary". After serving in the military for two years, she returned to university; started a bed-and-breakfast business while studying; worked at a listed company, and then transitioned into teaching. She initially thought she would continue her journey under the "teacher" halo. However, as rural revitalization evolved, the call for young power became loud and clear. With this expectation from her hometown, Zha Lisu returned to the village and became a "village official" under the identity of a "new youth of rural revitalization," transitioning from the cool "Teacher Zha" to the down-to-earth "Secretary Zha".

When the work environment shifted to her hometown, and her audience became her own neighbors, the young Secretary Zha did experience a bit of "culture shock".

But the charm and influence of youth lie in having a clear goal and moving forward without hesitation. The mix of "old, middle-aged, and young" village leaders formed the foundation for Zha Lisu to lead Daxi Village's cultural and tourism transformation. Her candid approach—putting issues on the table and discussing them openly with everyone—illustrates how she leads, while her careful planning, pragmatic execution, and management of rural development reveal the vitality that Daxi Village now enjoys.

"This year, our village team won the highest honor at the county's 'Practical Work Race', and more than half of the signed projects have already been implemented. Next year, the first 'Starbucks' in a rural area will open in Daxi Village, which will become a landmark event." She adds, "The countryside will always be the gentle foundation of the city and the future's greatest luxury. I hope it retains the warmth of nostalgia while bursting with youthful vitality."

It's hard to imagine that this is the "village secretary" who has only been in office for a year. "To be a village official, you need a spirit of dedication; without passion, you can't do it."

The mature and composed side of Secretary Zha is balanced by her personal time. With two days of exercise per week, seven days of vacation each year, and moments for reading and relaxation in between, Zha Lisu manages to carve out "myself" time—her version of a balanced rhythm in a "5+2" and "white+black" work schedule.

When asked about her name, she gives a playful smile: "I'm related to the famous Jin Yong, as 'Li' is my mother's surname. As for 'Su,' you'll have to ask my parents for that answer!"

**Keywords:**
Post-90s Village Party Secretary, New Youth in Rural Revitalization, Fitness Enthusiast

为了求学、为了生计，抑或是为了追求梦想而远离故土的青年啊，虽离家多年，但无论身在何方，心中那份对家乡的牵挂从未有丝毫减退。

当家乡开始发出呼唤，他们便有了踏上归途的内心回应。那熟悉又有些陌生的土地，那久违的温暖与安宁，安抚了游子的心，也激荡着年轻的血液润泽故土，令家园换上新颜。

# 归乡人
# 恋恋风尘，一生多少记挂

# *The Returnee: A Lifetime of Longing for Home*

For the sake of education, livelihood, or perhaps the pursuit of dreams, many young people leave their hometowns. Though years may pass and distances may grow, that deep connection to the homeland never fades.

When the call of home echoes, the heart responds. The land, familiar yet somewhat distant, the warmth and tranquility once forgotten, all serve to soothe the wanderer's heart. It stirs the blood of youth, renewing the homeland, and bringing forth a vibrant transformation.

# / 归乡，点燃星火 /

文 / 安然

归乡，对于许多青年来说，不仅仅是一次地理上的回迁，更是一次心灵的回归。

年轻的翅膀总是向往蓝天，心系远方。好像梦想的花朵总是长在更遥远的地方，而丁文文，却在辗转漂泊之后回到了熟悉的故乡。

2020 年，丁文文当时作为余村未来乡村验收服务负责人，来到这里以后，她有了新的思考：未来乡村验收工作是结束了，但是未来乡村的可持续发展要怎么继续？

带着这样的思索，她与当地政府工作人员不谋而合，利用这里的自然资源和文化特色，带上团队，带着青年人在这里“需求被听见、创意被看见、价值能变现”的核心理念，在 2022 年 7 月启动了首个“余村全球合伙人”计划，率先了开启“青年入乡”探索，目的便是疏通青年与乡村价值流动堵点，搭建一个青年与乡村价值双向流动、双向匹配的平台。

此后的三年，她带领团队成功吸引了余村全球合伙人、大学生、云村民来村创业创新。这些新鲜血液如星星之火点燃了余村，在余村的青山绿水之

关键词

安吉绿乡运营管理有限公司总经理 余村和“青来集”运营负责人 001 号余村全球合伙人

间发芽和生长，开出梦想的花朵。许多项目并不是“无根”的空降，而是结合乡村的现状，共同举办一些融合性的文化活动，推广传统手工艺，开设创业课堂。“青来集”不但成为青年创业的热土，也为“各自为战”的青年们创建了“数字游民基地”，为他们提供了一方栖息的天地，也为他们打碎了孤独。

丁文文说：“项目开启以来，成功招募了来自上海、湖州、杭州等地 20 余个合伙人团队入驻余村，现在常驻在村的青年有一千余人，已经孵化了 6 个余村子品牌，全网曝光量累计破亿。”数据之下，是这位归乡人对家乡深沉的爱。

## / Returning Home, Igniting Sparks /

For many young people, returning home is not just a physical reAddress, but a journey of the soul.

The wings of youth always yearn for the vast blue sky, with hearts set on distant horizons. It seems that the flowers of dreams are always found in faraway places. Yet, after years of wandering, Ding Wenwen returned to her familiar homeland.

In 2020, Ding Wenwen, then the leader of the Yucun Future Village acceptance service, came to the village and found herself pondering: While the work of future village acceptance had come to an end, how would the sustainable development of these villages continue?

With these thoughts in mind, she aligned with local government staff, leveraging the region's natural resources and cultural characteristics. Together with her team, she set out to create a platform where"needs are heard, creativity is seen, and value can be realized." In July 2022, she launched the first "Yucun Global Partners" program, initiating the "Youth Entering Villages" exploration. The goal was to clear the bottlenecks of youth and rural value flow, building a two-way platform for value exchange and matching.

In the three years since, she has led her team to successfully attract global partners, university students, and remote villagers to start businesses and innovate in the village.

These fresh minds have sparked a fire in Yucun Village, sprouting and growing among the lush mountains and waters, blooming with dreams. Many of the projects are not "rootless" initiatives; they are intertwined with the village's realities, hosting cultural events, promoting traditional crafts, and offering entrepreneurship classes. The "Youth to Rally" has not only become a thriving hub for youth entrepreneurship, but also created a "Digital Nomad Base" for youth to connect, offering them a space to belong and breaking the solitude many feel.

Ding Wenwen says, "Since the project started, we've successfully recruited over 20 partner teams from cities like Shanghai, Huzhou, and Hangzhou to join Yucun Village. Currently, more than 1,000 young people live in the village, and we have incubated six Yucun sub-brands. Our total online exposure has exceeded 100 million." Beneath these statistics lies the deep love of this returnee for her hometown.

**Keywords:**
General Manager of Anji Green Country Operations Management Co. Ltd. Operations Manager of Yucun and "Youth to Rally", No. 001 Yucun Global Partner

# / 让艺术美呼应乡村的自然美 /

文 / 安然

20 世纪 60 至 90 年代，中国动漫的天花板是《葫芦兄弟》《黑猫警长》《哪吒闹海》《舒克和贝塔》《大闹天宫》……由上海美术电影制片厂制作的上述动画片，其中的角色，如今在美在余村·国漫茶空间里经典再现。

这家国漫茶咖的负责人陈喆，从小就生活在这片土地上。长大后在上海读书和工作，2022 年 7 月，“余村全球合伙人”的招募呼唤，让他毅然选择放弃大城市的工作与生活，回到了这个熟悉的小乡村。他带着上海美影中国动画艺术 IP，带着国漫美学的文化内核，带着“首创乡村国漫茶咖项目”正式入驻余村，成为一名余村全球合伙人。

乡村与国漫的联结，是美学与乡村的联结。陈喆说这些动画形象的制作技艺，有水墨画、木偶、剪纸等传统的文艺形式，是中国美学的集成体现。他想要将这些东西以一种新的形式传递到中国乡村，传递给新一代的孩子们。

陈喆邀请了百年国民品牌马利颜料打造了疯狂画室；邀请了读者书店品牌来挖掘乡村文化，开展阅读大地的运营活动；邀请了豫园灯会品牌，联动中法文化交流的新春灯会，将竹子龙

**关键词**
**美在余村主理人　国漫文化创意人**

灯送去国际舞台；还邀请了隆庆禅院的悟澹禅师联合上美影VR开发团队，用传统儒释道的诠释和国学智慧对西游故事进行再创作……

“艺术的美总是高于自然的美”。国漫与乡村的结合，是一种艺术美与自然美的呼应。点一杯咖啡，闲坐在此，每一个到这里来的人，通过那些国漫形象，穿过时间的河流，或与记忆对话；或感受美，产生思考；又或者，还有一些什么正在心湖里荡起波澜，悄悄生长。

## / Let Art's Beauty Echo the Natural Beauty of the Countryside /

From the 1960s to the 1990s, the pinnacle of Chinese animation was embodied in iconic works like Hulu Brothers, Black Cat Detective, Nezha Conquers the Dragon King, Shuke and Beta, and The Monkey King. The characters from these beloved animated films, produced by the Shanghai Animation Film Studio, are now being revived in the "Beauty in Yucun" tea and coffee space.

Chen Zhe, the founder of this Chinese animation-themed tea and coffee space, grew up in this very land. After studying and working in Shanghai, in July 2022, he was drawn back to this familiar small village by the recruitment call for "Yucun Village Global Partnership Program" .He made the bold decision to leave behind his urban life and career, returning to his roots. Armed with the classic Chinese animation IP from Shanghai Animation Film Studio, a cultural core grounded in Guoji aesthetics, and the pioneering rural Guoji tea and coffee space project, he officially settled in Yucun village as a global partner.

The connection between the countryside and Chinese animation is a fusion of aesthetics and rural life. Chen Zhe explains that the production techniques of these animated characters—featuring traditional art forms such as ink painting, puppetry, and paper-cutting—are a profound expression of Chinese aesthetics. He envisions bringing these elements to the Chinese countryside in a new way, sharing them with the next generation of children.

Chen Zhe has collaborated with the century-old national brand, Maru Paint, to create the Crazy Studio; invited the Reader's Bookstore brand to explore rural culture and run educational activities; partnered with the Yu Garden Lantern Festival brand to introduce the bamboo dragon and lanterns to the international stage; and worked with Master Wuduan from Longqing Zen Temple and the Shanghai Animation Film Studio's VR development team to reinterpret the Journey to the West using traditional Confucian, Buddhist, and Taoist wisdom.

"Art's beauty is always greater than nature's beauty." The blend of Chinese animation and the countryside is a resonance between artistic beauty and the natural beauty of rural life. With a cup of coffee in hand, sitting in this space, every visitor, through the animated characters, is transported across the river of time, engaging with memories, contemplating beauty, or perhaps feeling ripples stirring quietly in their hearts, subtly growing.

**Keywords:**
Founder of Beauty in Yucun, Chinese Animation Cultural Creator

# / 理想艺术生活方式 /

文 / 枝枝

戴勋，1987 年出生，是个土生土长的上墅人。大学毕业后，他曾参加过国家足球青年队，后来在厦门一家旅游公司工作，正是在那里，他接触到了民谣。大约和年轻时候学习体育有关，戴勋的身上有着强烈的冒险精神。2016 年，安吉美丽乡村的名声越来越响，戴勋决定：回乡创业。

依托上墅乡优越的自然环境，他尝试将民宿、音乐和无公害农业相结合。当时，上墅一带的土壤被检测出富含微量硒元素，他开始种植富硒大米等无公害农产品，并萌生了打造自然牧场的想法。另一方面，戴勋开始投身民宿行业。他发现，老家附近闲置了十多年的乡卫生院背靠茶山，大院子里有棵巨大的百年香樟，很适合用来改造民宿。于是在 2017 年，由乡卫生院改造而来的大麓书院民宿正式运营。而后，他将摇滚民谣引入大麓书院，打造了安吉唯一一家以摇滚民谣为主题的民宿。

关键词
**大麓书院主理人　“音乐驻留计划”打造者**

戴勋像个拓荒者，在这片纯天然的土地上，用民宿、咖啡和民谣，开拓和培育上墅乡的音乐艺术土壤。树下咖啡正式营业后，不时举行音乐会、画展，表演插花、相声、蒙古草原音乐、脱口秀……有时是灯火流萤的夏夜，一支支歌谣穿破夜幕；有时是一个寻常日子的午后，屋子里传来欢声笑语；有时是一个静谧的雨夜，人同花草一起冥想，而后被疗愈。

人们一次次穿过村庄和田野，相会于此，以咖啡、歌谣、艺术和香樟的名义。这是独属于上墅的理想艺术生活方式。

## / The Ideal Artistic Lifestyle /

Dai Xun, born in 1987, is a native of Shangshu Town. After graduating from university, he briefly played for the national youth football team and later worked for a travel company in Xiamen. It was there that he was introduced to folk music. With a strong adventurous spirit, likely influenced by his sports background, Dai Xun made a life-changing decision in 2016, when the fame of Anji's beautiful countryside was growing: he chose to return to his hometown to start his own business.

Leveraging Shangshu Township's excellent natural environment, Dai Xun began to combine guesthouses, music, and pollution-free agriculture. At that time, the soil in the Shangshu Town area was found to be rich in trace selenium elements, so he began cultivating selenium-rich rice and other organic produce, while also developing the idea of creating a natural pasture. On the other hand, Dai Xun ventured into the guesthouse industry. He discovered that an abandoned rural health clinic near his home, nestled against tea mountains and with a massive century-old camphor tree in the courtyard, was an ideal site for conversion into a guesthouse. In 2017, the Dalu Academy guesthouse, transformed from the old health clinic, officially opened. Subsequently, Dai Xun introduced rock and folk music to the guesthouse, creating Anji's only rock-and-folk-themed accommodation.

Like a pioneer, Dai Xun cultivated the musical and artistic soil of Shangshu Town with guesthouses, coffee, and folk music on this pristine land. After the opening of Shuxia Coffee, various cultural events such as concerts, art exhibitions, flower arrangement performances, cross-talk, Mongolian grassland music, and stand-up comedy are held frequently. Sometimes, on a summer night lit by fireflies, songs cut through the darkness; sometimes, in the midst of a regular afternoon, laughter fills the air; sometimes, on a quiet rainy night, people meditate alongside the flowers and plants, finding healing.

People traverse the village and fields time and time again, gathering here in the name of coffee, songs, art, and camphor trees. This is the unique ideal artistic lifestyle of Shangshu Town.

**Keywords:**

Founder of Dalu Academy, Creator of the "Music Residency Program"

那些来自远方、带着不同文化和故事的人，因着一些机缘落在大余村这片土地上，或短暂或长期地留驻于此，慢慢扎根、焕发生机。初来乍到的新奇与陌生，随着时间的推移而消散，他们逐渐融入这片土地，触摸这里的过往，品尝这里的美食，见证也参与着这里的变迁与发展。他们不是局外人，而是同路人，与大家一起为这片土地注入新的活力与色彩。于他们而言，“吾心安处即故乡”。

# 外乡人
# 他乡，故乡

## *Outsiders: Foreign Lands, Hometowns*

People who come from distant places, bringing with them different cultures and stories, find their way to Da Yu Cun through various opportunities, whether for a short time or long-term. Over time, the unfamiliarity and novelty of their first arrival fade, and they gradually put down roots in this land, touch it's past, savor it's cuisine, and witness, and even participate in, it's transformation and development. They are not outsiders but companions on the same journey, injecting new vitality and colors into this land. For them, home lies wherever their hearts find peace.

# / 上海人在余村 /

文 / 朱寅

作为一个 80 后“户外探险达人”，张赟在不惑之年经历了深刻的自省与觉察。过去，张赟一直在上海从事品牌咨询和创业企业投资的事业，一切以企业效益为出发点。而现在，他深刻地意识到，除了经济效益之外，社会价值创造、人类文明进步、环境友好等同样重要，应该善用自己的行业资源和专业经验，促进共同富裕和可持续发展。

带着这样的信念，张赟来到了浙江省湖州市安吉县的余村——这里是“绿水青山就是金山银山”理念的发源地，不仅自然风光秀丽，而且地理位置优越，距离国际都市上海仅 200 多千米。

2022 年底，依托余村得天独厚的自然生态知名度与资源，张赟投资打造了高品质生态大米品牌“原力食品”。2024 年初，他又在余村投资创立了“青绿造物”这一生态 IP。“青绿造物”旨在以自身的品牌策划能力、产品设计能力、互联网销售能力，以大余村为资源基础，挖掘并塑造了一系列具有当地特色的乡村文创生态产品，并建立一个以大余村为中心、连接线上线下的绿色生活方式网络社区，吸引更多年轻朋友来体验乡村，甚至参与到乡村振兴的事业中来。成立以来，“青绿造物”在余村开设了第一家线下绿色文旅体验店余村邮局，如今已成为游客来到大余村景区内必打

**关键词**
**“原力食品” “青绿造物” 投资人**

卡的景点之一，并陆续引荐国际品牌 Timberland、HOKA 等来到大余村举办露营、徒步、越野跑等户外活动，让大余村越来越有国际范儿。

与此同时，张赟还积极为余村搭建与外部世界交流和沟通的桥梁。2022 年，他倡导发起“中国余村·国际绿色乡村发展论坛”，邀请来自世界 500 强企业的代表参观、访问和交流，为余村开辟了新的招商引资渠道；促成“哔哩哔哩”官方在余村设立“UP 主”乡村内容共创中心，鼓励创作有关绿色乡村和户外的优质内容，进一步展现推广余村的魅力。

让世界看到余村，让余村连接世界！张赟在乡村振兴和绿色发展的领域中乐此不疲。

## / A Shanghainese in Yucun village /

As an outdoor adventure enthusiast born in the 1980s, Zhang Yun underwent a profound self-reflection in his forties. In the past, he had always focused on brand consulting and investment in entrepreneurial ventures in Shanghai, where everything revolved around corporate profitability. However, he now deeply understands that, in addition to economic benefit, social value creation, the advancement of human civilization, and environmental friendliness are equally important. He believes in using his industry resources and professional experience to promote common prosperity and sustainable development.

With this belief, Zhang Yun arrived in Yucun Village, a village in Anji County, Huzhou City, Zhejiang Province—home to the concept "Lucid waters and lush mountains are invaluable assets." This village not only boasts beautiful natural scenery but is also strategically located, just over 200 kilometers from the international metropolis of Shanghai.

At the end of 2022, capitalizing on Yucun's exceptional natural ecology and resources, Zhang Yun invested in creating a high-quality ecological rice brand called "Yuanli Foods". In early 2024, he went on to establish Green Creation, an ecological IP in Yucun Village. Green Creation aims to leverage it's brand planning capabilities, product design, and internet sales abilities, using Da Yu Cun as a resource base to create and shape a series of local rural cultural and ecological products. It also strives to build a green lifestyle network community, both online and offline, centered around Da Yu Cun, attracting more young people to experience rural life and even participate in the rural revitalization movement. Since it's inception, Green Creation has opened it's first offline green cultural and tourism experience store, the Yucun Post Office, which has become one of the must-visit spots for tourists in the Da Yu Cun scenic area. It has also attracted international brands like Timberland and HOKA to host outdoor activities such as camping, hiking, and trail running in Da Yu Cun, giving the village an increasingly international flair.

At the same time, Zhang Yun has actively worked to build bridges of communication and exchange between Yucun Village and the outside world. In 2022, he initiated and organized the China Yucun International Green Village Development Forum, inviting representatives from Fortune 500 companies to visit and engage in discussions, opening new channels for investment and attracting business to Yucun Village. He also facilitated the establishment of Bilibili's official Village Content Co-Creation Center in Yucun Village, encouraging the creation of quality content related to green villages and the outdoors, further promoting Yucun's charm.

Let the world see Yucun Village, and let Yucun Village connect with the world! Zhang Yun is dedicated to rural revitalization and green development with great passion.

**Keywords:**
Investor of Yuanli Foods and Green Creation

# / 给每一条狗都取一个温暖的名字 /

文 / 安然

倪帅是一名留法建筑师，他说他来余村的目的是做一个乡村的观察者。学建筑的他，很快就迷上了这种乡村生活。

刚到村里时，倪帅发现村里有许多狗，于是便给每一条狗都取了一个名字，见面时就和它们打招呼。乡村生活的广阔，让人与人之间有着模糊的边界，人与小动物之间也有一种平等的亲切。没有人会因为是自己家的狗而纠正他取的名字，狗狗们也并不在意，一切都混沌又平和，温暖而不疏远。

后来倪帅的观察持续深入，把自己也放进大余村的氛围里，感受这里的一切。他去结交村里的手工艺人，给村民设计房屋；给村里的幼儿园重新设计更符合孩子需求的墙面色彩，还会到村里的学校去给孩子们上音乐课。多年来，他在乡村留下了一批批经典的设计项目：余村邮局、卫星工作室、好旺角民宿、菩提树下民宿、白术山下民宿、四正堂船村、船香竹宴、山川滑翔伞基地、溜索咖啡、山川乡人才大楼……

关键词
**独立建筑师　音乐爱好者**

热衷于自己动手完成设计的倪帅，在城市里未能实现的梦想也终于在大余村获得了圆满——他拥有了一间自己的木工房，并将对音乐的热爱，用匠心和巧手一一化作具象。他将回收来的旧木材做成各种乐器，如吉他、尺八、中阮、木琴、扬琴、古琴、三弦……还有许多新鲜的自创的发声器物。倪帅说：“我还有个乐队叫大象乐团，创作了很多歌，还没发过专辑，但应该也快了。”倪帅将自己的热爱，以一种轻快的方式，在大余村恣意地挥洒。大余村也回报他岁月静好，去享受、热衷于做一些寻常又温暖的事情。

## / Giving Every Dog a Warm Name /

Ni Shuai, an architect who studied in France, came to Yucun village with the intention of becoming an observer of rural life. As a student of architecture, he quickly became captivated by the simplicity of village life.

When he first arrived, Ni noticed there were many dogs in the village, so he decided to give each one a name, greeting them whenever he crossed their path. In this rural life, the vastness of the landscape created blurred boundaries between people, and there was an equality and warmth between humans and animals. No one corrected him for naming their dogs, and the dogs themselves didn't mind. Everything felt chaotic yet peaceful, warm without being distant.

As his observations deepened, Ni Shuai immersed himself in the atmosphere of Da Yu Cun, absorbing everything it had to offer. He befriended local artisans, designed homes for villagers, and reimagined wall colors for the village kindergarten to better suit the children's needs. He even taught music at the village school. Over the years, he left behind a series of iconic design projects in the village: the Yucun Post Office, Satellite Studio, Good Wangjiao Guesthouse, Under the Bodhi Tree Guesthouse, Baizhu Mountain Guesthouse, Fourfold Hall Boat Village, Chuanxiang Bamboo Feast, Shanchuan Town Paragliding Base, Liusuo Coffee, and the Shanchuan Town Talent Building, to name a few.

Passionate about hands-on design, Ni Shuai was finally able to fulfill a dream that he couldn't achieve in the city—he opened his own woodworking shop in Da Yu Cun. He turned his love for music into tangible creations, crafting instruments from reclaimed wood, such as guitars, shakuhachis, zhongruans, xylophones, yangqins, guqins, sanxians, and many other unique self-created sound-making devices. Ni Shuai shared, "I have a band called the Elephant Band. We've written many songs, though we haven't released an album yet, but it should be coming soon." He channels his passion into Da Yu Cun in a carefree, creative way. In return, Da Yu Cun gives him the peaceful passage of time, allowing him to enjoy and immerse himself in doing simple yet heartwarming things.

**Keywords:**
Independent Architect, Music Enthusiast

# / 深入乡村的肌理之中 /

文 / 樊多多

K.C 是安吉第一批数字游民，从 DNA（安吉数字游民公社）游到 DN 余村（余村数字游民公社），字母少了一个，却对安吉的了解更多了一层。两年三个月（截至 2024 年 8 月采访时）的入驻时间，让 K.C 与安吉产生了深度联系。

这些年来，K.C 内心保持着不曾被几十年的都市上班生活磨干净的童真，童真即好奇心，好奇心即我要探索这个世界。所以年轻时的陈先生北漂到京城，而后成为 K.C——Kevin Chen，做进出口工作，顺便深度游历北京以及全国大好河山。疫情给他高强度的工作踩了个小刹车，也让他循着大理的味儿到了安吉，成为 DNA（安吉数字游民公社）的内测人员之一，内测结束后他自然转正，成为数字游民。

在安吉，K.C 一部分时间分配给工作，该出差时出差，剩下的时间就是跑步和参与数字游民公社的运营工作，用他的话说就是“能不动就不动”，这里的不动，不是不运动，而是不外出。运动，特别是跑步，对于 K.C 来说非常重要，这是他探索大余村的方式。每个月 260 千米的跑量目标，不说跑遍大余村，也足以让 K.C 用脚步丈量的方式了解他所生活的这个地方。

**关键词**
**安吉第一批数字游民　乡村探索者**

K.C 不愿去定义或者刻意规划什么，但他总会在跑步的过程中接收到周围环境发给他的很多信号。比如他在天荒坪镇的大街上拍了 50 多个城市的车牌号。比如他在做天荒坪镇烧烤调研时，还顺便追溯了一下各村的迁移史，里面涉及了天荒坪、天子湖、梅溪、溪龙等乡镇最初移民的来处，就连村子里的徽派建筑遗存也仔细考察了一番，以上这些最终形成了一份活泼又严谨的文本。从中，可以读出他对生活在此地和身为“在路上”的数字游民的自洽与满足。

## /Immersed in the Fabric of the Countryside/

K.C is one of the first digital nomads in Anji. From DNA (Anji Digital Nomad Commune) to DN Yucun Village (Yucun Digital Nomad Commune), he dropped a letter but gained a deeper understanding of Anji. After two years and three months of residency (as of August 2024), he has formed a profound bond with this land.

Despite decades of urban corporate life, K.C has preserved a childlike curiosity—an insatiable drive to explore the world. In his younger years, Mr. Chen ventured north to Beijing, where he became Kevin Chen, navigating the import-export business while traveling extensively across China. The pandemic applied a sudden brake to his high-intensity work, nudging him toward Anji via Dali's bohemian allure. He became one of the beta testers for DNA and naturally transitioned into the lifestyle of a digital nomad.

In Anji, K.C divides his time between work—traveling when necessary—and engaging in the operations of the digital nomad community. As he puts it, he prefers to "stay still whenever possible"—not in the sense of avoiding movement, but in choosing not to leave his newfound home. Running is his way of exploring Da Yu Cun. With a monthly mileage goal of 260 kilometers, he may not have covered every inch of the village, but he has certainly traced it's essence with his footsteps.

K.C resists definitions and rigid plans, yet the world around him constantly communicates through subtle signals during his runs. He has casually documented over 50 different city license plates on Tianhuangping Town's streets. While researching the local barbecue culture, he also delved into the migration history of various villages, uncovering the origins of early settlers in Tianhuangping, Tianzihu, Meixi, and Xilong. He even meticulously studied the remnants of Hui-style architecture scattered throughout the village. These observations eventually culminated in a lively yet rigorous written record—one that reflects his harmony with life in Anji and his fulfillment as a digital nomad, always on the road.

**Keywords:**
The first batch of digital nomads in Anji, Rural Explorers

# / 神秘的自由译者 /

文 / 安然

这是一位我们未曾见到的余村外乡青年。

午后的“青来集”数字游民社区，时光似乎在这里慢了下来。我们去的时候，人并不多，偌大的办公区域在一片静谧之中。带着好奇与期待，去寻访一名在此地生活的自由译者陈正宇。

遗憾的是，他并未出现，他的朋友 K.C 表示他谢绝了我们的采访请求。他此刻就如天上那片云朵一样，遥不可及，又让人捉摸不透。于是，留给我们的，是一些神秘的遐想。

从他人的口中，我们得知他来自繁华的上海，带着一只叫王小咪的狗狗，选择了在这片宁静的土地上生活。他或许是厌倦了都市的喧嚣，或许是向往这里的宁静，又或许是追求一种更加自由的生活状态。总之，他选择了与山水为邻，与文字为伴。

手中刚好有一本他参与翻译的——《巴黎评论·短篇小说课堂》，我干脆翻出了他的那篇译作《除了有病我现在相当健康，没骗你》，我无法从评论者的角度做些评判，仅从一个读者的角度，我在他的文字里窥见了汉语的利落和美感。

我向来认为，译者是很伟大的存在，他们将一种语言转化为另一种语言，为世界文化搭建起沟通的桥梁。未曾谋面的陈正宇，或许是不想让我们打扰到他构筑桥梁的世界吧。

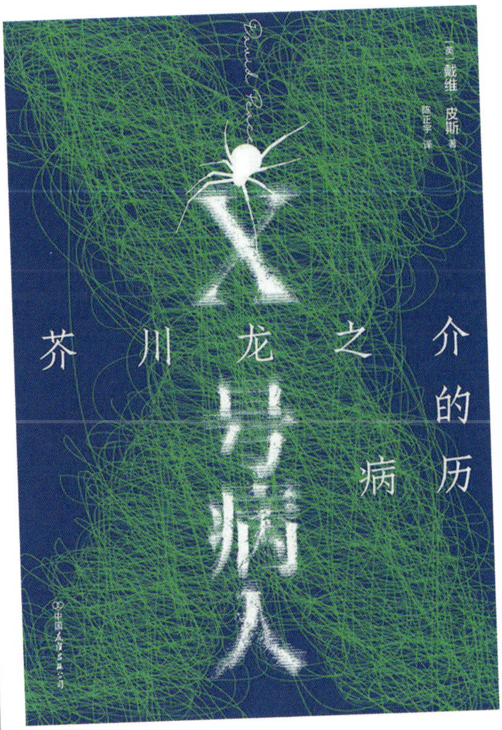

**关键词**
**文学爱好者　自由译者**

## / The Mysterious Freelance Translator /

He is a young outsider in Yucun village whom we have never met.

In the afternoon, at the Qinglaiji Digital Nomad Community, time seemed to slow down. When we arrived, there were only a few people scattered around, and the spacious co-working area was enveloped in quiet serenity. We came with curiosity and anticipation, hoping to meet the freelance translator Chen Zhengyu, who had chosen to settle here.

Regretfully, he did not appear. His friend, K.C , informed us that he had declined our interview request. At that moment, he felt as elusive as the drifting clouds in the sky—unreachable, enigmatic. And so, all that remained for us was an air of mystery and imagination.

From others, we learned that he hailed from the bustling city of Shanghai, accompanied by his dog, Wang Xiaomi. Perhaps he had grown weary of the city's clamor, or maybe he longed for peace, or sought a freer way of living. Whatever the reason, he chose to reside among the mountains and rivers, making words his lifelong companions.

By chance, I had a copy of a book he had contributed to—Object Lessons: The Paris Review Presents the Art of the Short Story. I turned to his translation of Except I'm In Perfect Health, No Kidding. I won't attempt to critique it as a reviewer; rather, as a reader, I caught glimpses of the sharpness and elegance of the Chinese language through his words.

I have always believed that translators are extraordinary individuals—they transform one language into another, bridging cultures and connecting worlds. Perhaps Chen Zhengyu, this translator we have yet to meet, simply wishes to remain undisturbed in the world of bridges he quietly builds.

**Keywords:**

Literary Enthusiast, Freelance Translator

# / 北来的雁，南国的家 /

文 / 元一

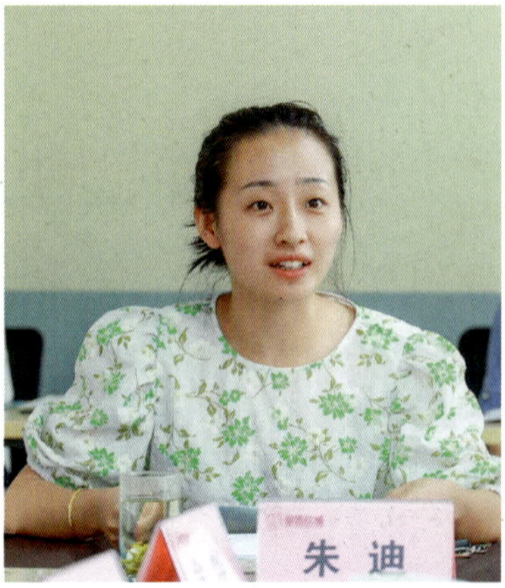

说起东北女孩朱迪和大余村的缘分，那确实是“从小”就有。

两三岁的懵懂时光，同伴们还在冰天雪地里打雪仗，朱迪就已经在天荒坪镇看江南天池的风光了。20 世纪 90 年代，父亲作为天荒坪抽水蓄能电站的建设者，把家人一起带到了这个南方小镇。直到回去上小学，朱迪的学龄前时光都是在天荒坪镇度过的。

连同儿时记忆一起带走的还有这里一位“叶舅舅”的疼爱，他是父亲在当地结识的好友。这段友情持续跨越二十载，最终在 2016 年升华，两家人因联姻紧密相连，朱迪这只娇俏的北雁成为余村媳妇，在南国安了家。

尽管南北生活习惯迥异，余村对朱迪而言，却总有股难以言喻的亲切感。这里既是她童年的梦幻之地，也是她如今的归宿。性情爽朗的她来到余村后便积极应聘村志愿者，为村民服务，深深融入余村。得益于与公公一家深厚的渊源，朱迪对余村的历史变迁有着深刻的理解并与之共鸣。沿着余村从矿业到绿色发展的生态之路，公公的工作从矿石运输到竹拉丝生意再到现在做休闲产业，每一次转型都映照出余村发展的轨迹。而在余村的岁月里，朱迪的角色也在不

**关键词**
**90 后村妇联主席　巾帼力量　乡村女子力**

断变换，从村团支部书记兼村史讲解员，到现任的村妇联主席，她一步步融入余村，成为一个地道的余村人。她以女性独有的细腻观察力、深厚的情感联结力和前瞻的创新思维，为余村的发展注入了新的活力与色彩。

“我从公公的身上看到余村绿色发展的道路，我在爱人的工作中感受到安吉转椅产业的蓬勃向前，我也在工作与生活的点滴里深深地感受、热爱着余村。”这是朱迪对余村最真挚的告白。

## / A Goose from the North, A Home in the South /

Zhu Di, a girl from Northeast China, has had ties to Da Yu Cun since childhood—quite literally.

In her toddler years, while her childhood playmates were still tossing snowballs in a frozen wonderland, Judy was already taking in the breathtaking views of Jiangnan Tianchi in Tianhuangping Town. In the 1990s, her father, a builder of the Tianhuangping Pumped Storage Power Station, brought the whole family to this southern town. For Judy, those carefree preschool years were spent in Tianhuangping, until she returned to the Northeast for elementary school.

Along with her childhood memories, she also carried with her the fond affection of "Uncle Ye," her father's close friend in the town. This bond endured for over two decades and reached a new height in 2016, when the two families were united by marriage. Zhu Di, like a delicate northern goose, found her home in the South as she became a daughter-in-law of Yucun village.

Though life in the North and South differs greatly, there has always been an indescribable sense of familiarity in Yucun village for Zhu Di. It was not only the dreamlike setting of her childhood but also the home she embraced as an adult. With her open and cheerful nature, she quickly became an active village volunteer upon arrival, wholeheartedly serving the locals and deeply integrating into the community. Thanks to her family's longstanding connection with the village, Zhu Di possesses a profound understanding of it's transformation over the years. From a mining-driven economy to an ecologically sustainable model, Yucun village has undergone remarkable change—a journey mirrored in her father-in-law's career evolution. Once engaged in mineral transportation, he later transitioned to bamboo filament production and now thrives in the leisure industry. With every shift, the village's development story unfolds. Likewise, Zhu Di's own role in Yucun village has continuously evolved. From serving as the village's Youth League secretary and historical narrator to her current position as the Women's Federation Chairwoman, she has become an integral part of the village. With the keen observational skills of a woman, an innate ability to foster deep emotional connections, and a forward-thinking mindset, Zhu Di has infused new energy and vibrancy into the village's growth.

"I see the path of green development in Yucun village through my father-in-law's journey. I feel the booming growth of Anji's swivel chair industry through my husband's work. And in every little moment of my life and work here, I have come to deeply love and cherish this place." These are the heartfelt words of Zhu Di—an inspiring woman, a leader of rural revitalization, and a true daughter of Yucun village.

**Keywords:**
Post-90s Women's Federation Chairwoman, Female Empowerment, Rural Women's Strength

# $O_2$生态文化圈

$O_2$ Eco - Cultural Circle

一座乡村的象牙塔，在群山的注视下，沐浴时光，山花烂漫。这是一个起帆之地，你飘逸的身影，青涩的脸颊，注定了一个美好的未来。

This is a place where the journey begins. Your graceful figure and youthful cheeks are destined for a wonderful future.

# 怀民亦未寝
# 不如一起啤酒伏特加

文 / 刘林

我为数不多的喝酒场合，有两种。

第一种是安静的小资酒吧。

灼热的夏日实在无处消遣，干脆和朋友参加了一个“酒鬼计划”——城市十多个酒吧共同组建的一个游戏：每个酒吧推选出两款鸡尾酒，参与者付钱即可以解锁任意三个酒吧前去品尝。

第一家，酒的口味不错；第二家，调酒师颇为热情，推荐了十数家他觉得值得一去的酒吧；第三家，酒嘛，难喝，环境嘛，还行，但有猫有狗，值了。

要说这个过程中，最大的乐趣是什么？大概就是奔赴下一家时，邻桌抛来“这么早就走了”的友好疑问，我表面娴熟地回一句：“哦，赶下一个场子。”内心却窃喜：嘻嘻，被我“装”到了——这是我第一次来酒吧。

第二种则是在喧闹的烧烤摊。

我与朋友相聚在这个场景下，多数是朋友发来郁闷的信息想要一醉解千愁。此时，一般喝的就是啤酒了。鸡尾酒适合小酌，闲聊之余，抿上一口；啤酒适合畅饮，多数时候是要伴随着激昂的脏话。毫不夸张地说，曾经有朋友请我吃烧烤喝啤酒，连续不停地吐槽了五个小时的工作。而我的内心毫无波澜，因为我知道，这就是被人请客的代价。

我一度觉得很神奇，当酒精进入我的夜生活之后，我才仿佛正式成为大人。大人，才有脑袋被酒精入侵后还能对自己负责的能力。或许享受不清醒，也是人生的一大乐趣吧。

Tips

# 来吧，与生活干杯！

## 乡音小馆

乡音小馆的前身是村里的一个垃圾站，用于堆放临时垃圾分类处理之用。2022年，85后主理人黄斌作为“余村全球合伙人”带项目进村，看中了这个地块的潜力，决定将其改造成酒馆。酒馆内部设计精巧，一层为乡村酒馆经营空间，兼具共享办公、品酒休憩、音乐交流等功能；二层则是乡村音乐人办公空间和乐队排练房。

🖂 天荒坪镇余村

## 老胡酒坊

老胡酒坊在余村的一条小巷内，颇有酒香不怕巷子深的风范。店内售有糯米酒、桂花酿、蜜桃酒、桑果酒、蓝莓酒、青梅酒、玫瑰酒、山楂酒等，价格都不贵，最贵的也不过 68 元一斤。

⊠ 天荒坪镇余村

## H2 角头街区

H2 角头街区在山川乡是由一幢老旧民房改造而来的，由返乡创业大学生和国内一流的调酒师共同打造。街区的主体外墙被粉刷成鲜艳的橘红色，带有浓郁的摩洛哥风格。采取“日咖夜酒”的经营模式，白天提供咖啡等饮品，夜晚则变成小酒吧，满足不同游客的需求。另外，这里也是一个机车驿站。

⊠ 山川乡山川村

## 顾氏酒坊&鲁昊酒厂

上墅乡间，一直以来亦有自酿白酒的习惯，在农村老百姓口中叫“吊酒”，他们用自家传统手工陶坛、陶缸发酵酿酒，再以陶坛贮存。其精心制作的白酒，口感纯正，风味独特，是不可多得的酒中极品。上墅人家自己酿酒不外乎两种方法：一是传统工艺，即选粮、泡粮、蒸煮、冷却、拌曲、发酵、蒸馏、出酒等工艺；二是新工艺，即选料（粮食、酒曲、水）、发酵（粮食 + 水 + 酒曲按比例混合搅拌）、蒸馏、出酒等工艺。上墅村的顾氏酒坊属于传统工艺酿造白酒的代表之一，罗村村的安吉鲁昊酒厂则是运用现代化工艺酿酒即生料酿酒的厂家。

⊠ 上墅乡上墅村（顾氏酒坊）；上墅乡罗村村（鲁昊酒厂）

## *Since Sleep Eludes Me, Why Not Share A Drink—Beer Or Vodka*

There are only a handful of occasions when I drink, and they fall into two categories.

The first takes place in quiet, sophisticated bars.

Scorching summer days often leave me restless, so one evening, my friends and I joined a "Boozers' Quest" —a city-wide drinking game organized by over a dozen bars. Each bar selected two signature cocktails, and participants, after paying a set fee, could unlock access to any three bars of their choice.

The first stop had great drinks; the second had an enthusiastic bartender who eagerly recommended over ten other must-visit spots; the third? The drinks were awful, the ambiance was decent, but there were cats and dogs—so it was worth it. But what was the most fun part of this adventure? Probably the moment when the neighboring table would throw a friendly, puzzled glance and ask, "Leaving so soon?" I'd reply smoothly, "Oh, just heading to the next spot." Meanwhile, deep inside, I'd giggle—Heh, they totally bought it. This was, in fact, my very first time at a bar.

The second kind of drinking happens at rowdy barbecue joints.

Most of the time, this happens when a friend sends a frustrated message, desperate to drown their sorrows in alcohol. This is where beer takes center stage. Cocktails are for light sips, a casual swirl between conversations; beer, on the other hand, is for gulping down—often accompanied by loud, passionate rants. I once sat through a five-hour, uninterrupted work-related rant from a friend who had invited me for beer and barbecue. And how did I feel? Completely unbothered—because I knew this was the price of a free meal.

It still amazes me how alcohol seemed to mark my transition into adulthood. Only adults, after all, can let their minds be invaded by liquor and still take responsibility for themselves. Perhaps, getting lost in inebriation is just another pleasure in life.

## Tips:

Cheers to life!

**Xiangyin Pub:** The Xiangyin Pub was converted from the village garbage station. The interior design of the tavern is exquisite. The first floor serves as the operating space of the rural tavern, integrating functions such as shared office space, wine tasting and resting areas, and music exchange venues. The second floor is the

office space for rural musicians and the rehearsal room for bands.
**Address:** Yucun Village, Tianhuangping Town

**Lao Hu Winery:** In the store, there are glutinous rice wine, osmanthus wine, peach wine, mulberry fruit wine, blueberry wine, green plum wine, rose wine, hawthorn wine, etc. for sale. The prices are not expensive. The most expensive one is only 68 yuan per jin.
**Address:** Yucun Village, Tianhuangping Town

**H2 Jiaotou Block:** The H2 Jiaotou Block is transformed from an old residential house. The main exterior wall of the block is painted in a bright orange-red color, exuding a strong Moroccan style. It adopts the business model of "coffee during the day and wine at night" to meet the needs of different tourists. In addition, it is also a motorcycle station.
**Address:** Shanchuan Village, Shanchuan Township

**Gu's Winery & Luhao Winery:** In Shangshu Township, the tradition of home-brewing white liquor has endured. The liquor here tastes pure and has a distinct flavor. The Gu's Winery represents traditional white liquor brewing techniques, while the Luhao Distillery employs modern raw material brewing methods.
**Addresss:** Shangshu Village ,Shangshu Township (Gu's Winery); Luocun Village, Shangshu Township (Luhao Winery)

# 离开孤岛计划

文 / 温瑶瑶

每天的清晨和傍晚，余村景区一片安宁。但是当工作时间来临，景区内的余村邮局、青年在村生活灵感便利店开始营业，人们都会在这里聚集起来。

在余村邮局最重要的是交流。余村邮局旁有火车样式的房间，这里不仅可以供人们举办活动时使用，也似乎是在喻示着在这里可以和世界各地交流。通过亲身经历，我看到，来到这里的人，都会走出属于自己的孤岛，和朋友、陌生人去交换着属于自己的故事。余村邮局与中国邮政有合作，你可以在这里将明信片寄出。

写下自己的故事，然后在满满的收获中离去。这里不仅仅有明信片，还有诸多关于大余村的文创产品。如果在余村邮局逛得不尽兴，可以再往东走上 1000 米，来到青年在村生活灵感便利店。猫猫是这里的守护神，也是招徕顾客的利器。而被猫猫吸引进去的人，往往会被更多的文创产品吸引注意。

在这些文创产品中，可以看到余村本来的模样和在各种文化冲击下的与时俱进的余村的模样。因为其独特性，我也出现过和友人玩石头剪刀布去争抢最后一个冰箱贴的情况，所幸是我赢了，其中的快乐比直接买到冰箱贴还要多上几倍。

当你离开余村时，寄出的明信片正在以相近的速度奔走到世界各地，你装进包里的收获也在不断向外散发着余村的味道和故事。这时你就会意识到，人生从来不是一座孤岛，走向余村，走向世界，都会有着更精彩的弧线。

## Tips

睁眼看世界已经不再是大城市人的专利，如今在像大余村这种乡村里，存在着许多卧虎藏龙的年轻人。于是，世界的眼光看向这里。甚至在这里，可以探索到别的地方都没有的超前设计！

**余村邮局：**有当地特产，也有最新潮的“外来物种”。各种元素和风格在这里融合，显示出一种“百花齐放”的氛围，让人流连忘返。

**青年在村生活灵感便利店：**一个充满设计灵感的小店，胸针、冰箱贴、徽章、明信片、手提包等形式的文创产品应有尽有，包括但不限于余村本地的特产和文化标志物、驻扎在余村的数字游民设计的作品等。除此之外，这里的景色也十分吸睛，店后面就是荷花池塘，旁边就是兜内咖啡，可以点一杯咖啡在便利店里坐坐。

**拾木工坊：**位于上墅乡，是一家致力于把木艺通过创新的方式融入现代人的生活的工坊，来到这里进行沉浸式体验，就可以忘记烦恼，还可以用一下午的时间亲手打造一件工艺品，物超所值。

## "Leaving the Island" Plan

Each morning and evening, Yucun Scenic Area is peaceful and tranquil. But when work hours arrive, the Yucun Post Office and the Youth's Life Inspiration Convenience Store in Rural Areas open their doors, and people gather here, creating a lively atmosphere.

At the Yucun Post Office, the most important thing is communication. Next to the post office, there is a small train-style room, which not only serves as a space for events but also seems to symbolize the idea that here, one can connect with people from all over the world. From personal experience, I've seen that everyone who comes here leaves their own isolated island behind, exchanging stories with both friends and strangers. The Yucun Post Office collaborates with China Post, allowing you to send postcards from here.

You can write your story on a postcard and leave with a sense of fulfillment. In addition to postcards, there are also many cultural and creative products related to Da Yu Cun. If you don't feel like browsing enough at the Yucun Post Office, you can walk another 1000 meters east to the Youth's Life Inspiration Convenience Store in Rural Areas. The cat, the guardian of this place, is also a marketing tool to draw customers in. Once inside, people often find themselves captivated by even more cultural products.

Among these creative items, you can see both the original form of Yucun and it's evolving shape under the influence of various cultures.

Due to their uniqueness, I've even found myself playing rock-paper-scissors with friends over the last refrigerator magnet, and thankfully, I won! The joy of winning was much greater than simply purchasing the magnet.

When you leave Yucun village, the postcards you sent will travel to destinations around the world at a similar speed. The treasures you've tucked into your bag will continue to spread the essence and stories of Yucun. At that moment, you'll realize that life is never an isolated island. Whether you're heading toward Yucun or the world, the journey will always create a more vibrant arc.

## Tips:

**Yucun Post Office:** It offers local specialties as well as the latest "foreign imports." Various elements and styles blend here, creating a "hundred flowers blooming" atmosphere that captivates visitors.

**Youth's Life Inspiration Convenience Store in Rural Areas :** A small shop filled with inspirational designs, offering a wide range of products such as brooches, fridge magnets, badges, postcards, handbags, and so on.The designs feature not only local specialties and cultural symbols of Yucun village but also works by digital nomads residing in Yucun village.

**Shimu Workshop:** Located in Shangshu, this workshop is dedicated to integrating wood art into modern life through innovative methods.

# 当我们在
# 音乐里醒来

文 / 温瑶瑶

在太平洋深处，博尔赫斯掷下一枚硬币，并为此写下了一首诗；十几年后，一位富商读到了这首诗，于是一场寻找太平洋中硬币的旷日持久的行动拉开帷幕。这场始于热爱的行动也许会被认为是疯狂的，但是也代表了一种人类为了追寻所爱而迸发出的炽热能量。这份爱，我在大余村也感受到了。

对于音乐最深沉的那份爱应当在大麓书院。那一年，在一棵大树下，一个

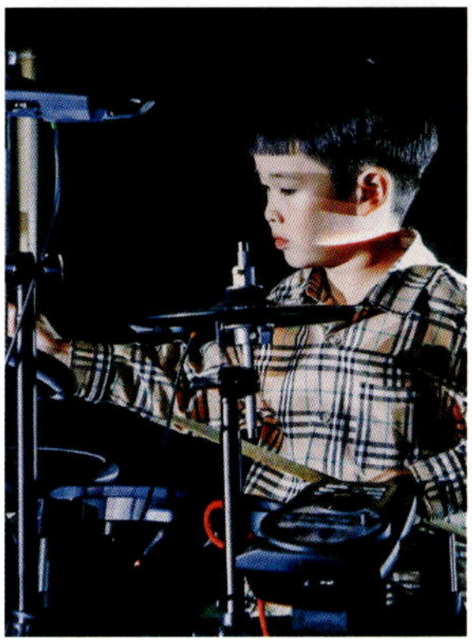

热爱音乐的人选择了这里。随着时间的流逝，钢筋、水泥、茅草、木头，共同构建起了一个家，一个属于音乐的家。于是大余村关于音乐的基因在这里慢慢孕育，随着不同工作室、独立人的入驻，衍生出了大麓音乐的品牌，在大余村，大麓逐渐成了音乐的一个代名词。大大小小的音乐节在这里举办，吸引了许多热爱音乐的人。

于是音乐就像蒲公英被吹散的种子一样，被散播到大余村的各个角落，如同在上墅乡的民宿中实行的一宿一器制度。还记得在一年前的某个下午，误入了上墅乡的我，走进了一家民宿，大堂有人在唱歌、弹吉他、弹琴。一曲终了，一问才知道，他们不过是素不相识的陌生人。我想这就是热爱的魅力，让富商和博尔赫斯联系在了一起，也让几个热爱音乐的素不相识的陌生人，出现在同一个空间中的同一首曲子里。

人们在这里聚集、互动，规划出一种属于大余村的音乐节，像一个个浮游因子，在大余村中游走。

Tips

## 大麓音乐

起源于安吉当地的大麓书院，以其极强的音乐性而延伸出来的品牌。至今在安吉已经举办过大大小小多次音乐节，每一次的人员阵容和场地都在拓展，给人一种不得不去的感觉。

## 一宿一器

以一定的标准，在上墅乡选择九家民宿，每家民宿根据自身特点和民宿主人意愿，选定一件乐器。乐器选定后，民宿老板要先学会演奏该乐器，增加与客人的互动。比如浣溪沙民宿的非洲鼓、锦艺民宿的古筝、云竹谷民宿的扬琴、溪旅民宿的尤克里里等。

## 音乐人

在安吉境内，还有许多独立的音乐人和乐队，其中有的是本地人，有的是从外面来到安吉的。每种音乐都有着自己独特的视角和特色，听过之后就会知道，安吉的音乐世界精彩纷呈。

1. 戴勋：戴勋是上墅人，在工作中接触到了民谣音乐，经过几年的忙碌后，终于在 2016 年，决定回到安吉从事音乐事业。他的音乐可以被分类为摇滚民谣，有着十分鲜明的上墅特色。

2. 沈健：安吉孝丰人，从小受电视、广播中音乐的熏陶，到了大学便开始和志同道合的朋友一起组建乐队，也举办了个人演唱会。毕业后沈健就留在安吉从事音乐相关工作，是安吉当地具有代表性的独立音乐人。

3. 低苦艾乐队：中国民谣摇滚的开山乐队，2003 年成立于兰州，成员共有 6 名，其作品有着很高的艺术价值与强烈的人文关怀，曾多次在大麓书院进行演出。

# Waking Up in Music

Deep in the Pacific, Borges once tossed a coin into the sea and wrote a poem about it. Years later, a wealthy businessman read that poem, sparking a long and relentless search for the coin. This quest, born from passion, might be deemed madness, but it represents the fiery energy humans unleash when pursuing what they love. This love is something I've also felt in Da Yu Cun.

The deepest love for music can be found at Dalu Academy. That year, under a tree, a music lover chose this place. Over time, steel, concrete, straw, and wood came together to form a home—a home for music. Slowly, the musical spirit of Da Yu Cun began to take root here. As various studios and independent artists moved in, the Dalu Music brand emerged, and in Da Yu Cun, Dalu became synonymous with music. Small and large music festivals are now held here, drawing music lovers from all around.

Music, like dandelion seeds, is scattered across every corner of Da Yu Cun, much like the "one night, one instrument" system practiced in the homestays of Shangshu Town. I remember a year ago, on a quiet afternoon, I wandered into a homestay in Shangshu Township, where I found people singing, playing the guitar, and the piano in the lobby. After the song ended, I learned they were strangers to one another. This is the magic of passion—it links a businessman to Borges and brings together music lovers who've never met, united by the same song in the same space.

Here, people gather and interact, planning a music festival unique to Da Yu Cun. Like floating particles, music moves through the village, creating a vibrant, shared experience.

## Tips:

**Dalu Music:** From Anji's Dalu Academy, this brand hosts diverse music festivals in Anji, expanding in lineup and venue, creating a must-attend atmosphere.

**One Homestay, One Musical Instrument:** According to certain criteria, nine homestays were selected in Shangshu Township. Each homestay would choose one musical instrument based on it's own characteristics and the wishes of the homestay owner.

**Musicians in Anji:**
① **Dai Xun:** A Shangshu native, he pursues a music career in Anji, creating rock-folk music with Shangshu characteristics.

② **Shen Jian:** He grew up with music and became a representative independent musician in the area after graduation.

③ **Di Kuai Band:** A Chinese folk-rock pioneer formed in Lanzhou in 2003, their works are artistically valuable and humanistic.

# 夜观天象，找出个喝咖啡的**好时机**

文 / 温瑶瑶

古代在皇宫中，有个职位叫太卜，日常的工作内容就是夜观天象，卜算良辰吉时。

一来大余村，我感觉自己就化身成了太卜，掐指一算，就算出了在此地喝咖啡是一个天时、地利、人和的大好时机。

所谓天时。众所周知，咖啡是打工人早上八点的“续命水”。大余村一游，脱离了工作日的拘束，咖啡不再是拿在手中、步履匆匆间猛吸一口提神的“物料”，而是摇身一变成了一种享受。咖啡豆产地在哪儿、手冲还是特调、花香还是果香……平时懒得研究的东西，顷刻间都让我产生了雅兴。

再谈地利。安吉咖啡馆的崛起，似乎就是这一两年的事情。时间虽短，却精彩纷呈。或是坐落于绿水青山之间，或是与当地文化结合，或是承载了一些特殊情感理念，唯有大余村这片土地方才能赋予它施展空间。

最后是人和。在大余村与咖啡馆邂逅，实则是与每个咖啡馆主人有趣的灵魂相遇。在与他们的畅聊之中，我自己也变得比平时更雀跃了一些。

一路从余村喝到上墅再喝到山川，成就了我一场丰富的咖啡体验之旅。不用掐指算，我就知道，下次我肯定还是要来的！

## Tips

山水为邻，醇香四季。咖啡的诱惑不只在于香浓、纯粹和调制的变化，更在于手持一杯醇香咖啡时所处的环境、所感受到的意境。余村咖啡世界，各种意想不到的风味和此间真意，邀你来体验。

### 天池观景 Coffee

一处“天选”观景的咖啡店，在这里，与朋友、爱人静静地坐着，欣赏窗外的美景，闻着咖啡的香味，能找到内心的宁静和满足。如果赶不上观赏凌晨的日出和傍晚的日落，还有触手可及的星星在等着你。

推荐：香草拿铁、锤锤水蜜桃

🖂 天荒坪镇大溪村江南天池景区游客中心旁

### 瀑布咖啡（星空营地版）

这是一个露营浪漫计划捕捉地——“安吉摘星星的地方”。在这里，可以一边露营，一边看星星，一边品味咖啡。

推荐：拿铁、摩卡

🖂 天荒坪镇大溪村香炉自然村038号-2

### 溪西里 River Park Coffee

在溪边，倾听竹林和风的窃窃私语，聆听潺潺溪水与石头的碰撞声音。喝着一杯泰式风味的饮品，仿佛置身清迈的绿荫里。

推荐：泰式风味相关饮品

🖂 天荒坪镇横路村赤坞里南633米

### 青之恋舍 Cafe & Tea

青之恋舍以咖啡为主打饮品，老板娘是咖啡爱好者，亲自制作咖啡并调配口味。咖啡口感香醇浓厚，令人回味无穷。咖啡厅旁边还有一个银杏公园，闲来可以去游逛一番。

推荐：美式咖啡、燕麦拿铁

🖂 天荒坪镇余村两山景区天荒坪路

## 葡萄叔叔的猫咖馆

天荒坪银坑村路口的那家葡萄园，宠妻的老板把自己的葡萄园重新改造，给喜爱养猫的老板娘打造了一个“撸猫咖啡”店。

推荐：特调 + 撸猫套餐

✉ 天荒坪镇安吉青创农业股份有限公司园区内

## 与余农场 Fun Coffee

以亲子田园沉浸式体验为核心，打造一个“原汁原味”的农场，是一家田园风光十足的咖啡店。买一杯咖啡，即可入场享受萌宠围绕的快乐生活！

推荐：拿铁、卡布奇诺

✉ 天荒坪镇年年有余研学中心酒店东南 100 米

## 瀑布咖啡（巴厘岛版）

咖啡馆后共有三级天然瀑布，山野的瀑布美景与咖啡屋结合，成为这处咖啡空间的独特性。嬉戏玩水，赤脚坐在溪流中踩着石头喝咖啡的感受，你一定没试过！

推荐：拿铁、龙井奶茶、椰子水

✉ 山川乡大里村秧田坞自然村 88 号

## 美在余村国漫茶咖空间

在这个空间，童心被唤醒，儿时看过的国漫主角围绕在身边，头顶轮播着那些经典动漫画面，恍惚童年从未远去，童心未泯，梦想永在。

推荐：由孙悟空、黑猫警长、舒克、贝塔、葫芦娃等掌管的咖啡、红茶、白茶、冰激凌，任君选择。

✉ 天荒坪镇余村印象青年图书馆

## 大麓书院树下咖啡

名副其实开在大树下面的小咖啡馆，院子里的大树是整个场域的核心。这是一个以音乐为主题的休闲艺术空间，咖啡是音乐的搭档，放松是生活的向往，田野之内，艺术之外，你我共鸣。

推荐：宿醉拿铁、椰汁美式、啤酒美式、香草拿铁

✉ 上墅乡上墅村文昌阁自然村

## 山边边咖啡馆

窗外的田园风光、老牛，法式农村的悠闲与慵懒在一杯咖啡里慢慢呈现。享受从前慢的好时光就是如此简单。

推荐：葡萄冰萃美式

✉ 上墅乡罗村村大坝路旁

## *Stargazing for the Perfect Coffee Moment*

In ancient times, there was a palace position called the "Taibu," whose job was to observe the stars at night and calculate auspicious times.

When I first arrived in Da Yu Cun, I felt as though I had transformed into that very Taibu, calculating the perfect time to enjoy a cup of coffee.

First, there's the timing. As we all know, coffee is the life-sustaining beverage for office workers at 8 am. But in Da Yu Cun, away from the constraints of the workweek, coffee isn't just a quick sip on the go to stay awake. Instead, it becomes an experience to savor. Questions like the origin of the beans, whether it's hand-brewed or a specialty blend, and the floral or fruity notes—things I usually never bother to consider—suddenly become intriguing.

Then, there's the address. The rise of cafes in Anji seems to have been a recent phenomenon, but in such a short time, they have flourished in many creative forms. Some are nestled among the lush mountains and rivers, others blend local culture into their offerings, and some

even carry emotional or philosophical significance. Only the land of Da Yu Cun could provide the space for these cafes to thrive.

Lastly, there's the people. My encounters with the cafe owners in Da Yu Cun were like meeting fascinating souls. In our conversations, I felt a sense of joy and excitement that went beyond my usual self.

From Yucun Village to Shangshu Town and then to Shanchuan Town, my coffee journey became a rich and fulfilling experience. No need for calculations— I already know I'll be back next time!

## Tips:

Neighboring mountains and rivers offer a rich aroma year-round. Coffee's charm extends beyond flavor, purity, and brewing methods, embracing the ambiance and mood. Yucun Coffee World invites you to discover its delights.

- **Tianchi Viewing Coffee:** It's a coffee shop blessed with a perfect viewing spot.
  **Recommendations:** Vanilla Latte, Hammer Peach.
  **Address:** Next to the Tourist Center, Jiangnan Tianchi , Daxi Village, Tianhuangping Town

- **Waterfall Coffee (Starry Sky):** Camp, stargaze, and sip coffee.
  **Recommendations:** Latte, Mocha.
  **Address:** No. 038-2, Xianglu Natural Village, Daxi Village, Tianhuangping Town

- **Xixili River Park Coffee:** By the stream, enjoy Thai-flavored beverages.
  **Recommendations:** Thai Drinks.
  **Address:**633 meters south of Chiwuli, Henglu Village, Tianhuangping Town(Navigate to Xixili River Park Coffee)

- **Love of Green Cafe & Tea:** The female boss is a coffee lover. She makes coffee by herself and adjusts the flavors.
  **Recommendations:** American Coffee, Oatmeal Latte.
  **Address:**Tianhuangping Road, Liangshan Scenic Area, Yucun Village, Tianhuangping Town

- **Uncle Grape's Cat Cafe:** Vineyard-converted cat cafe.
  **Recommendations:** Special Blends, Cat-petting Package.

**Address:** Within the Park of Anji Qingchuang Agriculture Co., Ltd., Tianhuangping Town

- **Fun Coffee at Yuyu Farm:**
Farm-based cafe for parent-child experiences.
**Recommendations:**
Latte, Cappuccino.
**Address:**100 meters southeast of Niannianyouyu Research and Study Center Hotel, Tianhuangping Town

- **Waterfall Coffee (Bali):**
Natural waterfalls behind. Enjoy coffee with barefoot in the stream.
**Recommendations:**
Latte, Longjing Milk Tea, Coconut Water.
**Address:** No.88, Yangtianwu Natural Village, Dali Village, Shanchuan Township

- **Comic Tea & Coffee Space:**
Chinese animation-themed cafe.
**Recommendations:** Coffee, Tea, Ice cream.
**Address:** Yucun Impression Library, Tianhuangping Town

- **Dalu Academy Tree-Shaded Coffee:** Under a big tree, themed around music.
**Recommendations:** Overnight Latte, Coconut Milk Americano, etc.
**Address:** Wenchangge Natural Village, Shangshu Village, Shangshu Township

- **Hillside Cafe:**
French countryside ambiance.
**Recommendations:** Grape Iced Americano.
**Address:** Beside the road of the Dam, Luocun Village, Shangshu Township

# 与绿水青山互联，去除“班味”

文 / 王偶得

我觉得自己应该是个 ESFJ（MBTI 人格类型之一）。因为在听到余村有 500 多个大自然工位时，我竟然打心底里产生了向往。

产生这个念头大致可以说明三个问题：一、我不喜欢城市里写字楼环境下的办公状态；二、我喜欢亲近大自然，跟山林花鸟风在一起；三、我不介意在大自然的环境里办公。鉴于以上三点，我判断自己是一个喜欢工作的人。

喜欢工作的人也可以分两种吧，一种是为自己工作，一种是为老板工作。但其实如果豁达、通透一点，都可以认为是为自己工作。有个网络名词叫“社畜”。“社畜”这个词里大概包含着三分调侃、三分无奈、四分“悲催”的意味。还有一个词叫“班味”，指打工人特有的疲惫气质。我不太具有理解网络流行语的脑回路，但我深深理解这两个词背后的意味。但是，不管为谁工作，开心是一天，不开心也是一天，那为啥不心花怒放地工作与生活呢？比如此刻的我，正坐在大自然工位上流畅地码下以上文字。

Tips

大自然工位，源自安吉大余村的创新理念，旨在将乡野自然与现代工作方式巧妙融合。利用大余村丰富的自然资源和多元的空间，创造出一个既充满活力、创造力，又充满生命力的自由办公创业场域。

大自然工位分为移动式、风景式和沉浸式三类，提供桌椅、无线网络、充电设施等基础办公设施，避雨、取暖等增值服务可在服务驿站和服务盒子找到，还可以提供一键报警、一键就医、一键报修功能，显示附近共享自行车、电动车租借情况，推荐附近餐饮住宿，并提供电子地图以显示各类工位使用情况和配套标准。

## Connecting with Nature, Saying Goodbye to the "Workplace Vibe"

I think I must be an ESFJ (one of the MBTI personality types). When I heard that Da Yu Cun has over 500 nature-inspired workstations, I found myself genuinely attracted to the idea. This thought reveals three things about me: first, I don't enjoy working in the city office environment; second, I love being close to nature, surrounded by mountains, forests, and wildlife; third, I don't mind working in a natural setting. Based on these points, I can confidently say I enjoy working.

There are two types of people who enjoy working: those who work for themselves, and those who work for their boss. But, if you take a more open-minded view, you could say we're all working for ourselves. There's an internet term called "office drone," which blends humor, helplessness, and a bit of "misery." Another term is "workplace vibe," referring to the tired, worn-out atmosphere that office workers often embody. While I don't always keep up with internet slang, I understand the meaning behind these terms. But no matter who you're working for, why not choose to enjoy your day—whether working or living? For example, here I am, sitting at a nature-inspired workstation, happily typing these words.

## Tips:

The "Workstation in Nature" is an innovative concept originating from Da Yu Cun in Anji. It aims to skillfully integrate the rural natural environment with modern working styles. By making use of the abundant natural resources and diverse spaces in Da Yu Cun, it creates a dynamic, creative and vibrant free workspace for office work and entrepreneurship.

The "Workstation in Nature" is divided into three types: mobile, scenic and immersive. It provides basic office facilities such as desks, chairs, Wi-Fi and charging facilities. Value-added services like protection from rain and heating can be found in the service stations and service kiosks. It also offers functions such as one-click alarm, one-click medical service and one-click maintenance request. It can display the rental status of nearby shared bicycles and electric vehicles, recommend nearby dining and accommodation options, and provide an electronic map showing the usage status and supporting standards of various workstations.

# 阅读

## 随身携带的小型避难所

文／刘林

“阅读——随身携带的小型避难所”，当这个标题和我的名字放在一起时，仿佛这句话的作者是我。实则不是，它是英国作家毛姆说的。而我，还没看过毛姆的作品。

冒昧“盗用”一位我并不熟悉的作者的名言，或许正是源于和他一样能在阅读中寻得一方天地的共鸣。

这种共鸣，是忙碌的七月，读到了科幻大师雷•布拉德伯里《夏日遇见狄更斯》，随着狄更斯的旅程，工作的焦躁和夏日的烦闷被清扫；是在虚无主义中怀疑世界，遇见萨特、波伏娃后，被“存在主义是一种人道主义”所治愈；是第一次翻开《太古和其他的时间》，被托卡尔丘克笔下八十四块时间裂片拼贴出的历史斑斓大梦所惊艳……

博尔赫斯曾写过一个短篇，名为《巴别图书馆》。在他的畅想之中，世界的核心是一个巨大的图书馆，每一本书都是宇宙的碎片，知识的海洋浩瀚无垠，却又充满了未知的重复与变异，令人沉迷又不断追寻其中。

于是，我也幻想过自己是一个图书馆管理员，或是一个书店店员，不必为经济所累，每日优哉游哉地翻着喜爱的书籍，不那么尽心尽力地向借书人或顾客介绍我喜爱的书籍。推荐的第一本书，或许就是博尔赫斯短篇合集《阿莱夫》。毕竟，我真的看过博尔赫斯的书。

Tips

## 大余村的精神避难所在哪里？

### 1. 余村印象青年图书馆

这是一座由水泥厂改造而成的乡村图书馆，它不仅融合了工业记忆与乡村生态，还集书籍阅览、乡村文创、教育研学、文艺展陈等多个功能区于一体，藏书丰富，是当地乡村阅读与文化交流的重要场所。来了记得去一楼“凡有所爱，皆是青年——在余村，青年被重新定义”的标语旁打卡拍照。

⊠ 天荒坪镇余村

### 2. 青年在村生活灵感便利店

店里投放了许多供免费阅读的文学书籍，可在旁边的兜内咖啡店买杯咖啡，随手翻开一本图书，静坐一个下午。

⊠ 天荒坪镇余村

### 3. 大麓书院书店

书店坐落在大麓书院内。

⊠ 上墅乡上墅村大麓书院内

### 4. 云下湖畔图书馆

图书馆在云下湖畔拥有一栋自己的小建筑，内里的图书是之前云下湖畔与村内举办的活动募捐而来的。如果有缘来到云下湖畔，可以去逛一逛这个图书馆。

⊠ 山川乡云下湖畔内

# Reading: A Portable Refuge

When the title "Reading as a Portable Refuge" is paired with my name, it almost feels like I am the author of this quote. In reality, it was said by the British writer William. Somerset Maugham. I haven't read any of Maugham's works yet.

Perhaps my audacity in "borrowing" a quote from an author I am not familiar with stems from the resonance I feel with his ability to find solace in books, just as he did.

This resonance occurs in busy July days when I read Ray Bradbury's Summer Meeting, and alongside Dickens' journey, my anxieties from work and the summer heat are swept away; it happens when, in a world filled with existential doubt, after meeting Sartre and Simone de Beauvoir, I find solace in the notion that "existentialism is a form of humanism"; it occurs when, for the first time, I open Primeval and Other Times by Olga Tokarczuk and am stunned by the vibrant historical dreams pieced together from eighty-four fragments of time.

Borges once wrote a short story called The Library of Babel, imagining a world where the core is a vast library. Every book in it is a fragment of the universe, the ocean of knowledge is boundless yet filled with unknown repetitions and variations, leaving one endlessly fascinated and searching for more.

I too have fantasized about being a librarian or a bookstore clerk, free from financial worries, leisurely flipping through my favorite books. Instead of working tirelessly to recommend books to borrowers or customers, I would simply share the ones I love. The first book I would recommend might just be Borges' The Aleph, because, after all, I've actually read Borges' works.

## Tips:

Where are" the refuges"in Da Yu Cun ?

**1.Yucun Impression Youth Library**
This is a rural library transformed from a cement factory.It integrates functions such as book reading, rural cultural creativity, educational research, and literary exhibitions. With a rich collection of books, it is an important venue for rural reading and cultural exchange.
**Address:** Tianhuangping Town,Yucun Village
**2.Life Inspiration Convenience Store**
The store offers many literary books for free reading. You can buy a cup of coffee, pick up a book, and sit quietly for an afternoon.
**Address:** Tianhuangping Town,Yucun Village
**3.Dalu Academy Bookstore**
The bookstore is located within the Dalu Academy.
**Address:** Dalu Academy, Shangshu Village, Shangshu Township
**4.Yunxia Lake Library**
The library has it's own small building aside Yunxia Lake. If you happen to be at Yunxia Lake, take a stroll to this library.
**Address:** Within Yunxia Lake, Shanchuan Township

在悠远的笛音里，我听见一位舞者在春风里呢喃，仿佛沈复与芸娘流连溪畔。芦苇开始返青了，你的足迹清晰可见，又是一个春天。

In the distant sound of the flute, I hear a dancer whispering in the spring breeze. The reeds are starting to turn green again, and your footprints are clearly visible. It's another spring.

# 人文弧光

Splendid Humanities

# 化身为马，参加一场中式 Cosplay 大赏

文 / 元一

2024年除夕那天，我在安吉大余村与“活”了几百年的灯有个约会，一起参加一场中式 Cosplay 大赏。在这个光影重重、五色斑斓、锣鼓喧天的日子，我将自己化出两个分身，一为关公，一为马，只有两条腿的马。

大赏以“出灯！”为号令，一声令下，各路马灯有序出场。骑着枣红马的关公，也就是我，站在队伍的最后，观赏、审视着正在加入这支大部队的有灵万物：马、鳌、鱼、彩贝、蝴蝶、龙凤、金童等，可谓是天上人间，囊括海内。像我这种跨越时空、活跃至今的历史人物或小说角色还有樊梨花、杨宗保、穆桂英、孙悟空等，都是带着英雄标签、有忠义担当的。他们和我一样身着戏曲中的经典服饰，脸上有妆，赏灯观众一看到我们的扮相就能对号入座，并将我们的形象、所处朝代和故事绘声绘色地告诉身边的儿孙，典型的中华传统文化实地研学。

眼前四角阵、龙门阵、梅花阵、元宝阵等几个阵型如走马灯似的轮番上演。嗯，是名副其实的马灯，外形如马，内里骨架是竹，表面覆着的彩纸或绸布在马身灯光的映照下显出更高的色彩饱和度，这样的色彩总是让人身心愉悦。

我一直关注场中，直到场地对角线那头“皇嫂”的身影出现，我便按捺不住胸中激情，催动胯下这匹和我的面庞一样枣红色的“马”，千里走单骑，开启一场护卫之旅，正如这缤纷的大余村竹灯，穿越几千年，依然如此鲜活。

Tips

大余村的马灯主要集中在山川乡山川村、天荒坪镇大溪村、上墅乡龙王村和董岭村，均入选湖州市级非物质文化遗产名录。在安吉方言里用“调”来表达灯会开始，调灯，即出灯表演。灯会表演多是人们祈求风调雨顺、五谷丰登、平安吉祥、家庭安康的朴素表达形式，是中华传统民俗艺术的优秀代表，也是人们勤劳智慧与创造力的结晶。春节至元宵期间来安吉大余村，可以欣赏到大溪村调马灯、山川村竹马灯、山川村鳌鱼灯、西坞花灯、董岭花灯等马灯表演，感受独特的节日氛围和传承不衰的非遗魅力。

## *Transformed into a Horse, Joining a Traditional Chinese Cosplay Extravaganza*

On the eve of the 2024 Lunar New Year, I made an appointment with lanterns that had "lived" for centuries in Anji's Da Yu Cun, participating in a grand Chinese cosplay celebration. On this day filled with dazzling lights, vibrant colors, and the clamor of drums, I became two characters: Guan Yu and a horse — a horse with only two legs.

The grand event began with the command "Out with the lanterns!" At the signal, various lanterns paraded out in an orderly fashion. I, dressed as Guan Yu riding a chestnut horse, stood at the end of the procession, observing and examining the parade of lively lanterns: horses, turtles, fish, seashells, butterflies, dragons, phoenixes, and golden children — a true feast for the eyes, bridging heaven and earth. Historical and literary figures like Fan Lihua, Yang Zongbao, Mu Guiying, and Sun Wukong, who like me, carry the heroic labels of loyalty and duty, joined the procession. Dressed in traditional opera costumes and painted faces, we became living symbols of classic Chinese tales, allowing the audience to easily recognize us and recount our stories and historical periods to their children and grandchildren — a vivid, hands-on experience of traditional Chinese culture.

The lanterns performed in various formations, such as the Four-Corner Array, Dragon Gate Array, Plum Blossom Array, and Ingot Array, each more mesmerizing than the last. The lanterns were shaped like horses, with bamboo frames and colorful paper or silk coverings that shimmered brightly under the lantern light, offering a satisfying visual feast.

I remained focused on the spectacle until I spotted the figure of "Empress" at the far end of the field. Unable to contain my excitement, I urged my chestnut-colored horse, just like my own face, into a gallop. The journey began — a protective ride, much like the vibrant lanterns of Da Yu Cun, which have crossed millennia and still glow brightly.

## Tips:

The horse lanterns in Da Yu Cun are mainly concentrated in Shanchuan Village of Shanchuan Township, Daxi Village of Tianhuangping Town, Longwang Village and Dongling Village of Shangshu Township. All of them have been included in the list of Huzhou Municipal Intangible Cultural Heritage. In the Anji dialect, the word "diao" is used to indicate the start of the lantern fair. "Diao Deng" means the performance of the lanterns going out. The lantern fair performances are mostly simple expressions of people's prayers for favorable weather, bumper harvests of grains, peace, good luck, and the well-being of their families. They are excellent representatives of traditional Chinese folk art and also the crystallization of people's hard work, wisdom and creativity. During the period from the Spring Festival to the Lantern Festival, when you come to Da yu cun in Anji, you can enjoy the performances of horse lanterns such as the Tiao Ma Deng in Daxi Village, the bamboo horse lantern in Shanchuan Village, the Ao Yu lantern in Shanchuan Village, the Xiwu flower lantern, and the Dongling flower lantern, and feel the unique festival atmosphere and the enduring charm of the intangible cultural heritage.

# 当一个“不求心”的愚者

文 / 朱寅

2023年遇上了一连串不顺心的事情。项目中遇到大难题，我便去首都某个大庙祈福。为此我还排了一小时队，斥巨资请了条据说能保佑事业顺利的手串。回到杭州，惊闻——项目没了！同事们笑得不行，都说你这香烧得太“灵光”了！

最近这几年，我也开始学着上香了，遇到古庙必上香，唯求心安和顺利。

听说余村的后山就有座千年古刹——隆庆禅院，始建于五代后梁，是吴越王钱镠亲自建造，后来几经修葺扩建。虽说是一座山寺，但几乎不用爬山，沿村里的绿道缓步向上，到达半山平台，便是禅院的主建筑。禅院隐藏在群山竹海中，来余村旅游的人很多，但这座寺庙却出奇的安静。寺庙随处可见岁月的痕迹，一步一景，漫步院内，远眺山峦，清风徐来，好不自在！

遗憾的是，我去的那天，住持悟澹法师外出，寺中只有一个种菜的志愿者大叔看家。听说住持还是位青年作家，本想向他讨教下《红楼梦》，再听听他讲的禅修课。或许还可以再来一次，放下心中杂念，体验一番脱离尘世的轻松。

本地朋友介绍，安吉还有座千年古刹——石佛寺，据说许愿很灵验，但要爬灵溪山。翻过两座山头，远远看见青翠的山林中掩映着黄墙黛瓦。寺中偶遇一位年长的女信徒，她告诉我经常来庙里当义工。据说石佛寺每次翻修，所需的建材都是靠人力肩挑背扛运上山来的。直到前几年有了索道，僧人们才终于有机会修了个装空调的接客室。

这几年，每到一处寺庙，我都会“请”一条漂亮的手串，如今已实现可以半个月不重样的手串自由了。名义上是为了祈福，实际上还是满足自己对首饰的欲望。然而无论是隆庆禅院，还是石佛寺，都找不到法物流通处。我失望地询问石佛寺的师父，他只是笑着摇摇头，穿过那道明代遗留下的石门，缓步离去。

那一刻，我意识到自己到处搜集手串的行为有多么肤浅！或许，我被浮躁的消费主义裹挟，所求的不外乎发财、事业有成，我早就失去面对物质得失时的那份从容淡定。

不过转念一想，也不必太苛责自己。网络流行语说，当代年轻人，在上班和上进之间选择上香；在做牛和做马之间选择做法！其实，上香也是一种积极上进的体现。上香的人至少对未来怀有渴望和期待。面朝佛像点燃佛香的那一刻，只是为了暂时逃离现实的压力；通过虔诚的一拜，获得一丝心灵的慰藉和力量。

下山时正好是下午 5 点，我们赶上了景区最后一班接驳车，司机把景区电瓶车开出了秋名山车神的漂移感，打工人要下班的快乐溢于言表。我似乎有所领悟。“圣人求心不求佛，愚人求佛不求心。”与其求神拜佛，不如修炼自己，少些物欲才能找到简单的快乐。至少，努力不当那个“不求心”的愚者。

Tips

## 大余村的古刹余韵

**1. 石佛寺**

进入灵溪景区之后，爬山大约 15 分钟后抵达索道，索道直达石佛寺，免去至少 1 小时的登山之苦。入院可领三支香；寺院提供斋饭素面，可以询问师父。

**2. 隆庆禅院**

始建于五代后梁，几经修葺扩建。位于余村后山，不用门票，几乎不用爬山。沿村里的绿道缓步向上，到达半山平台，便是禅院的主建筑。也可骑共享单车上山。

**3. 化度寺**

位于上墅乡大麓书院附近，化度寺原本年代久远，但近些年来做了些翻新工作。如果到大麓书院饮茶喝咖啡，不如顺便踱步来这里逛逛。

# Becoming a Fool Who "Does Not Seek the Heart"

In 2023, I faced a string of unfortunate events. When a major issue arose in one of my projects, I went to a famous temple in the capital to pray for blessings. I waited in line for an hour and spent a small fortune on a bracelet said to ensure career success. Upon returning to Hangzhou, I was stunned to hear—the project was gone! My colleagues couldnt stop laughing, saying my incense had worked"too well"!

In recent years, I've started to light incense myself. Every time I encounter an ancient temple, I offer incense, seeking peace of mind and smooth progress.

I heard that there is a thousand-year-old ancient temple, Longqing Zen Monastery, located on the back mountain of Yucun village. It was originally built during the Later Liang period of the Five Dynasties and was personally constructed by King Qian Liu of Wuyue. The temple, which has been renovated several times, is tucked away in the bamboo forests of the back mountains. Although it's a mountain temple, there's no need to climb a steep slope—just a leisurely walk up the village's green path leads to the main buildings on the mid-mountain platform. The monastery is remarkably quiet, even though many visitors come to YuCun Village. The traces of time are evident everywhere within the temple, with scenic views at every turn.

Walking through the courtyard, looking out over the mountains, a gentle breeze brings a sense of tranquility.

Unfortunately, the abbot, Master Wuduan, was out the day I visited, and the only person there was an elderly volunteer tending to the garden. I had heard that the abbot was also a young writer, and I had hoped to seek his insights on Dream of the Red Chamber and attend one of his Zen meditation classes. Perhaps I could return someday, let go of my distractions, and experience the serenity of the temple.

Local friends told me about another ancient temple in Anji, Shifo Temple, known for it's effective blessings, but to get there, one has to climb Lingxi Mountain. After crossing two mountain ridges, I finally saw the temple nestled among the lush green forest, it's yellow walls and dark tiles barely visible from afar. There, I met an elderly female devotee who told me she often volunteered at the temple. She explained that the materials needed for repairs were once carried up the mountain by hand until a cable car was installed a few years ago, allowing the monks to finally build a reception room with air conditioning.

Over the past few years, whenever I visit a temple, I always "acquire" a beautiful bracelet, and now I can go half a month without repeating a single one. Officially, it's for the sake of blessings, but in reality, it's more about satisfying my desire for jewelry. However, whether at Longqing Zen Temple or Shifo Temple, I couldn't find any place selling Buddhist items. Disappointed, I asked a monk at Shifo Temple about it. He simply smiled, shook his head, and, without saying a word, walked slowly through the stone gate, a relic from the Ming Dynasty.

In that moment, I realized how shallow my habit of collecting bracelets had become! Perhaps I've been swept up in the frenzy of consumerism, seeking wealth and success. I've long lost the calm and composure I once had when facing the gains and losses of material things.

But then I thought, there's no need to be too harsh on myself. A popular saying among young people is that between working and striving, I choose praying; between being a beast of burden, I choose conjuring spells. In truth, lighting incense is also a form of striving. Those who offer incense at least hold some hope and expectation for the future. The act of lighting incense before a Buddha statue is, for a moment, an escape from the pressures of reality. Through a sincere bow, one seeks a small consolation and strength for the heart.

On the way down, it was just 5 pm, and we caught the last shuttle bus of the day. The driver took the electric car down the mountain with a drifting flair reminiscent of the famous Akina Mountain God of Drift. The joy of workers leaving their shifts was palpable. I think I've learned something: "The sage seeks the heart, not the Buddha; the fool seeks the Buddha, not the heart." Rather than seeking gods and Buddha statues, it's better to cultivate oneself. By reducing material desires, one can find simple happiness. At the very least, let's strive not to be the fool who "does not seek into the heart."

## Tips:

Remember to visit these three temples in Da Yu Cun

1.Stone Buddha Temple

The Stone Buddha Temple can be reached by a 15-minute hike up the mountain followed by a cable car ride, saving you at least an hour of trekking. Upon entry, you will be given three incense sticks, and the temple offers vegetarian meals and noodles; feel free to inquire with the monks.

2.Longqing Temple

Built during the late Liang dynasty of the Five Dynasties period, the Longqing Temple has undergone several renovations and expansions. It is located on the hill behind Yu Cun, and admission is free.

3.Huadu Temple

Located near Dalu Academy in Shangshu Township, Huadu Temple is originally an ancient site but has undergone some renovations in recent years. If you're here at Dalu Academy for tea or coffee, why not take a leisurely stroll over to this place for a visit?

# 龙王古道
## 也无风雨也无晴

文 / 刘林

我在平原上长大，对山向来是敬畏之中带着一丝抗拒。原因无非是我不善爬山，无法乐在其中，也无法欣赏时光赋予山中古道的深厚人文积淀，显得非常“可恶”。于是造就了在龙王村阴山古道的起点会合之时，友人们要么一脸沉稳要么一脸跃跃欲试，而我一脸无奈的滑稽场面。

我们并不是专业的背包客，因此特意请了常常上山的村民帮忙，由他们用绳子将打包好的露营装备捆牢，再挂在竹竿的两头扛在肩上，像旧时翻山运货一样，靠这种传统的方式将装备运上山。

我无从想象先人那一往无前的勇气从何而来，只知道对于我来说，上山可真不是一件容易的事。我缺少锻炼的身躯是战略的先天不足，背包里装了一堆重且无用的电子产品是战略的后天决策失误。

我就像歌里唱的那样“翻山越岭，却无心看风景”，还迫于无奈无师自通地发明了“狗爬式”爬山法——四肢并用爬着上山，简直就是字面意义上的“像狗一样”。

行至半山腰，我们寻到了一块野餐的好地方。在一个凉亭旁，有一块完全背阴、临近水源的空地。一小番忙碌之后，眼前的一片空间俨然成了我们的小天地。村民们吃着三明治、火腿肠，喝着家酿的土烧。友人与村民们交谈，听他们讲古道

过去的故事，同他们分享我们带过来的零食与水果。

我无暇参与讨论，一心埋头猛吃。吃着吃着却想到，明明村民是为帮忙上山而来，我们则奔着登高野餐与露营而来，但此时此刻，围坐在一起的我们好似却并没有什么区别。难怪佛家常说凡所有相皆是虚妄，世间万物众多表现形式的背后，都有相同的本质。

莫名地，就在这一刻，我忽然想通了。古道的本质无非就是旧人走过的路，它不会言语，又怎么会怪罪于我？霎时，我心中原本对于古道的敬畏与抗拒消散了大半。

我平视了古道，也坦然接受了自己的平庸与不解风情。

## 龙王古道推荐路线

龙王古道全长约 29 千米，大致可分为：大岭古道、欢喜岭古道、回峰岭古道、阴山古道、蓑衣塘古道。

**1. 回峰岭—蓑衣塘古道环**

路程：2.4 千米 平均坡度：26.19° 难度：低

最大海拔落差：310 米 时长：1.5 小时

**2. 阴山—大岭古道环**

路程：3 千米 平均坡度：22.20° 难度：低

最大海拔落差：423 米 时长：2.5 小时

**3. 回峰岭—欢喜岭古道环**

路程：4.2 千米 平均坡度：20.00° 难度：中

最大海拔落差：401 米 时长：3.5 小时

**4. 欢喜岭—蓑衣塘古道环**

路程：4.5 千米 平均坡度：19.80° 难度：中

最大海拔落差：402 米 时长：4 小时

**5. 欢喜岭—大岭古道环**

路程：5.6 千米 平均坡度：17.20° 难度：中

最大海拔落差：472 米 时长：5.5 小时

**6. 回峰岭—大岭古道环**

路程：7.5 千米 平均坡度：15.90° 难度：高

最大海拔落差：500 米 时长：7 小时

**7. 阴山—蓑衣塘古道环**

路程：8.5 千米 平均坡度：17.19° 难度：高

最大海拔落差：571 米 时长：8 小时

## The Longwang Ancient Path: Neither Wind Nor Rain, Nor Sunshine

I grew up on the plains, where I always held a mix of awe and subtle resistance towards mountains. The reason was simple: I wasn't good at climbing and could never find joy in it, nor could I appreciate the deep cultural heritage built up along the ancient paths of the mountains. This made me feel rather "irritating." So, when we gathered at the starting point of the Yingshan Ancient Path in Longwang Village, my friends either wore calm expressions or looked eager to begin, while I had a face full of helplessness.

We weren't professional backpackers, so we asked local villagers, who frequently climbed the mountain, to help. They used ropes to securely bundle our camping gear and carried it on bamboo poles, much like how goods were transported in the old days, bringing everything up the mountain with this traditional method.

I could hardly imagine the bravery of our ancestors, but I knew that for me, climbing a mountain was no easy feat. My body, unaccustomed to exercise, was a natural disadvantage, and my backpack, filled with heavy and useless electronics, was a strategic misstep. As the song goes, "Climbing mountains and crossing ridges, but with no interest in the scenery," I invented my own "dog-crawl" method of climbing—using all fours to crawl up the mountain, literally like a dog.

By the time we reached halfway up, we found a good spot for a picnic. Next to a pavilion, there was a shady patch of land near a water source. After a bit of work, the area seemed to transform into our little world. The villagers ate sandwiches and sausages, sipping homemade wine. My friends chatted with the villagers, listening to their stories about the ancient path, while sharing the snacks and fruit we had brought.

I had no time to join the conversation, as I was too focused on devouring the food. As I ate, I couldn't help but think—though the villagers came to help us climb, and we came for the hike, picnic, and camping, at this moment, we didn't seem so different after all. It suddenly struck me that Buddhism often says that all appearances are illusions, and behind the many forms of the world lies the same essence. In that moment, I had an epiphany. The ancient path was nothing more than the road walked by those before us. It didn't speak, so how could it blame me? My earlier awe and resistance toward the ancient path faded away.

I looked at the path with a calm gaze, accepting both the path and my own mediocrity and lack of appreciation for finer things.

## Tips:

Recommended routes for the Longwang ancient path

Climbing in autumn, the LongWang Ancient Route group is a good choice, with a total length of about 29 kilometers, roughly divided into: Daling Ancient Route, Huanxiling Ancient Route, Huifengling Ancient Route, Yinshan Ancient Route, and Suoyitang Ancient Route.

**1.Huifengling-Suoyitang Ancient Route Loop**
Distance: 2.4 km; Average Slope: 26.19 °; Maximum Elevation Difference: 310m; Difficulty: Low; Duration: 1.5 hours

**2.Yinshan-Daling Ancient Route Loop**
Distance: 3.0 km; Average Slope: 22.20 °; Maximum Elevation Difference: 423m; Difficulty: Low; Duration: 2.5 hours

**3.Huifengling-Huanxiling Ancient Route Loop**
Distance: 4.2 km; Average Slope: 20.00 °; Maximum Elevation Difference: 401m; Difficulty: Medium; Duration: 3.5 hours

**4.Huanxiling-Suoyitang Ancient Route Loop**
Distance: 4.5 km; Average Slope: 19.80 °; Maximum Elevation Difference: 402m; Difficulty: Medium; Duration: 4.0 hours

**5.Huanxiling-Daling Ancient Route Loop**
Distance: 5.6 km; Average Slope: 17.20 °; Maximum Elevation Difference: 472m; Difficulty: Medium; Duration: 5.5 hours

**6.Huifengling-Daling Ancient Route Loop**
Distance: 7.5 km; Average Slope: 15.90 °; Maximum Elevation Difference: 500m; Difficulty: High; Duration: 7.0 hours

**7.Yinshan-Suoyitang Ancient Route Loop**
Distance: 8.5 km; Average Slope: 17.19 °; Maximum Elevation Difference: 571m; Difficulty: High; Duration: 8.0 hours

# 来都来了，那就带点什么走吧

文／刘林

中国人向来信奉一句话：来都来了。每每去旅游总是要带点伴手礼走，证明本人“到此一游”。时间久了，却也发现有些所谓的“土特产”，在购物软件上搜同款一搜一个准，"世界义乌"岂是说说而已？所以说，伴手礼，也是分个三六九等的。

在我眼里，那些与土地紧密联系的民俗风物是最高级的，因为它们是伴手礼界的“可遇不可求”。

它们深植于一方水土，承载着那片土地的历史、信仰、审美与智慧。每一件民俗风物背后，都藏着一个动人的故事，一段悠久的历史，一种独特的文化表达。这种深度与广度，是千篇一律的流水线上生产的物件难以企及的。

Tips

## 丨大余村的“可遇不可求”有哪些？

### 1. 天荒坪竹刻

安吉竹刻技艺创始于清末，手艺人巧妙地运用阴线、阳刻、圆雕等多种手法，在竹制的器物上雕刻出各种装饰图案和文字，或用竹根雕刻成各种陈设摆件，展现出独特的艺术魅力。在天荒坪镇，安吉竹刻不仅作为地方特色旅游产品受到游客喜爱，更是成了一张具有鲜明地域特色的文化名片。

### 2. 罗村斗笠

安吉地处江南，每逢绵绵细雨时节，种田人家都离不开斗笠。几乎每家每户都有斗笠。小小斗笠，既能遮阳，又能挡雨，神通广大。上墅乡罗村双盘头自然村 20 世纪 70 年代之前出生的人，基本都会编织斗笠。一把篾刀，一个帽楦，一张帽板，用竹篾夹油纸或竹叶棕丝就能编织成一顶顶朴实的斗笠。如今罗村斗笠已成为县级非物质文化遗产，常常参与非遗主题的展示、展演活动。

### 3. 龙王造纸年画

上墅乡龙王村手工造纸至今已有百年历史，晒干的竹制纸，色泽土黄，具有吸湿性强和燃烧完全的特点。2008 年村里为了拓展手工造纸用途，从武强引进了年画制作技术。龙王造纸非遗传承人章亚红为了寻求手工造纸作坊的发展出路，将古老技艺和传统创意结合了起来——在龙王纸上创作丰富多样的年画。如今，很多游客来龙王村，会来体验龙王年画，并把亲手做的一张张年画带回家。

### 4. 山川山袜

“天不怕地不怕，媳妇就怕做山袜。”山袜在山川乡有着悠久的历史，其传承历史已无从考证，但据当地老人回忆，这种袜子是他们祖辈世代相传的劳动用品。山袜有点像京剧里面武生的中筒薄底靴。通体米色，袜底大概一两厘米厚，袜头圆润微微上翘，袜底和袜筒连接处看得出有厚厚的绲边。在生活富裕物质丰富的今天，山袜成了一种独特的文化遗产，安静地待在安吉五坊六艺展示馆的橱窗里。

### 5. 请自己挖掘吧

旅行的一大意义，就在于自行探索，或是从溪边捡起的一小块石头，在大树下捡起的一片落叶，或是与这个地方的人产生一段对话、聆听一个小故事，都可以是“可遇不可求”的上等伴手礼。当自己亲身参与其中，就已经与这片土地产生了关系。

站在马路的起点，山的轮廓在蓝天的映衬下清晰可见，庄严静穆。它一直就在那里，与村庄和人们，长久地在一起。

Standing at the starting point of the road, the outline of the mountain is clearly visible against the backdrop of the blue sky, solemn and serene. It has always been there, staying with the village and the people for a long time.

# *Come All the Way, So Take Something With You*

The Chinese have always believed in the saying: "Come all the way, (so take something with you.)" Whenever we travel, we're inclined to bring back some souvenirs as proof that we've been there. Over time, however, I've realized that many so-called "local specialties" can be easily found online with a quick search. Isn't the "World's Yiwu" more than just a saying? Therefore, souvenirs can be divided into different tiers.

In my eyes, the highest-tier souvenirs are those closely tied to local customs and traditions, as they are the "once-in-a-lifetime" gems of the souvenir world.

These items are deeply rooted in the land they come from, carrying the history, beliefs, aesthetics, and wisdom of the region. Behind each folk artifact is a captivating story, a long history, and a unique cultural expression. This depth and breadth are beyond what mass-produced, standardized items could ever match.

# Tips:

What are the "unexpected treasures" in Da Yu Cun?

### 1.Tianhuangping Bamboo Carving

Originating in the late Qing, Anji's bamboo carving uses diverse techniques. It's a favored tourist item and cultural symbol in Tianhuangping.

### 2.Luocun Bamboo Hats

In rainy Anji, bamboo hats are essential. People in Luocun's Shuangpantou (born before the 1970s) can weave them. Now a county - level intangible heritage, they often appear in cultural events.

### 3.Longwang Paper - making New Year Pictures

Longwang Village's paper - making has a 100 - year history. The paper is absorbent and burns well. In 2008, New Year picture skills were added. Tourists like making and taking them home.

### 4.Shanchuan Mountain Socks

In Shanchuan, these socks, like Peking Opera boots, have a long history. Now a cultural relic, they're displayed in the Anji Five Workshops and Six Arts Exhibition Hall.

### 5.Explore Yourself

Travel means self - discovery. A pebble, a leaf, or a chat can be precious. Your participation connects you to the land.

鲲鹏驭风，扶摇九万里，新的桃花源正在这里出现。
陶渊明虽老，在此东篱种菊却也十分惬意。

A new Peach Blossom Spring is emerging here. Even though Tao Yuanming has long passed away, the place where one could plant chrysanthemums by the eastern fence here seems as boundless as the realm he envisioned.

# 玩转四季

## The Beauty of Four Seasons

# 春天，
# 去找一朵花

文 / 温瑶瑶

对于热爱着生活的人来说，春天是一个最值得寻觅的季节。不管是山间生长的野菜、野草、野花，还是人为努力培育出来的一片片花田，都向人们展示了春天这个季节的性质——无畏地生长。

这是我们初入大余村的第一个春日清晨，来到了天荒坪镇的五鹤村。薄雾尚未消散，还笼罩着清晨析出的露水。春天于我来说像是一幅水粉画，一切颜色都是柔和的，没有一个明确的边界，直到一块小小的梯田上，一片黄色闯进我的眼睛。如果这种颜色出现在日常生活中的没有生命的物体上，许多人会觉得艳俗而刺眼，但是当它们涂抹在成片的田地里时，顿时就给人以不同的感受。这就是生命的魔法。

寻找了越多的花就越会知道，颜色是这种花朵最不起眼的特色之一，它们在环境设置的重重阻碍中不管不顾地生长着，一朵花如何盛开，如何吸收阳光，如何往更深的泥土里扎根，如何在寒冷的夜晚闭合，这些花朵背后的故事，似乎远比盛开那一刹那的美丽更值得探究。

于是在经过一个春天的观赏与收集后，可以确定地说，在晴空万里时我的第一选择就是去找一朵花。

## 玉兰花

春日里沿着罗董线一路往北，路边尽是优雅的白玉兰在风中摇曳。白玉兰的花苞大而洁白，开花后花瓣丰盈、花色洁白、造型极为华丽，无怪乎古人赞其“天谴霓裳试羽衣”。

## 樱花

在平常的农家小院旁，也可以找到些零散的春意；但是想要赏樱，较为集中的地点是江南天池旁，新开放的樱花大道（樱雨路），让人全方位处于春天的美好之中。

## 桃花

春天正是桃花盛开的时候，在大余村内，有许多地方适合观赏桃花，较为著名的是江南天池旁。

## 油菜花

在天荒坪镇五鹤村树景坞自然村内就有一片种满油菜花的梯田，到了油菜花盛放的季节，这里连成一片花海，十分夺目。

## 映山红

四月，是山川乡灵溪山风景区漫山的映山红盛开的季节。来灵溪山风景区，沿着山路欣赏这些野蛮生长的红花，颇有一番意趣。

## In Spring, Go Find a Flower

For those who love life, spring is the season most worth seeking out. Whether it's the wild herbs, grasses, and flowers that grow in the mountains, or the fields of flowers carefully cultivated by humans, all of them showcase the essence of spring — a fearless desire to grow.

On our first spring morning in Du Yu Cun, we arrived at Wuhe Village in Tianhuangping Town. The mist had not yet dissipated, still clinging to the dew settled by the early morning. Spring, to me, is like a watercolor painting, where every color is soft, with no clear boundaries. But then, on a small terraced field, a patch of yellow broke into my view. If this color appeared on an inanimate object in daily life, many would consider it gaudy or glaring. But when it's painted across vast stretches of land, it gives off an entirely different feeling. This is the magic of life.

The more flowers you search for, the more you come to realize that color is one of the least remarkable features of these flowers. Despite the obstacles set by their environment, they grow relentlessly — how they bloom, how they absorb sunlight, how they root deeper into the earth, how they close up in the cold night. The story behind these flowers seems far more fascinating than their fleeting beauty in full bloom.

So, after a spring of observation and collection, I can confidently say that on a clear day, my first choice is to find a flower.

## Tips:

**Magnolias:** As you travel north along the Luodong Road in spring, you will find elegant white magnolias swaying in the wind along the roadside.

**Cherry blossoms:** The newly opened Cherry Blossom Avenue (Yingyu Road) beside Jiangnan Tianchi, where you can immerse yourself in the beauty of spring.

**Peach blossoms:** In Dayu Village, there are many places suitable for viewing peach blossoms, with the more renowned address being beside the Jiangnan Tianchi (South of the Yangtze Heavenly Lake).

**Rape flowers:** In Shujingwu Natural Village, Wuhe Village, Tianhuangping Town, there is a terrace field planted with rape flowers.

**Azaleas:** April is the season when azaleas bloom across the Lingxi Mountain scenic area in Shanchuan Township.

# 夏日入侵企划!

文 / 安然

夏天最佳的避暑胜地，不是海滨小城，不是沙滩和太阳伞，而是大山腹地，给你一个湖，一挂瀑布，一场漂流，你就会在这里度过一段丰富而热烈、安宁又清凉的夏日时光。

大余村湖多，它们大多四面环山，湖水静谧清幽，在青山的映衬下不顾炙烤的骄阳，每个湖都和它本身一样，散发着深不见底的魅力。这里无主的“野湖”很少，无论它如何沉默，岸

边总是散落着各种业态以及各项围绕着湖泊而开发的各类激情四射的水上项目。

抵达星潮营地的时候，一群小学生正在湖边进行桨板的下水前训练，年轻帅气的教练不厌其烦地用语言和肢体示范着正确的桨板操作，对桨板一无所知的我们，乖巧得像个小学生，在一旁默默蹭课：前进、定桨、倒退……跪式、站式、半立式……

理论课学好了，上桨板时还是忐忑，救生员在一旁轻描淡写地安慰我说：落水是正常的。他不说还好，这一说，我的恐惧又多三分。不由得又看了一眼拴在脚上的安全带，脑子里全是落水时，我要如何利用这条安全带逃出生天的画面。拴在脚踝处，真的管用吗？万一掉下去头朝下，脚在上，要如何自救？

恐惧归恐惧，上了桨板，理论加实践的方式，让我很快就找到了感觉，前进、后退、三板定桨！我玩得不亦乐乎。

人与桨板微妙的互动和平衡，在屡试不爽之后，很容易会将人与桨板的互动，误会成一种单方面的驾驭能力，从而滋生出一种“人桨合一”的狂妄豪情：从湖边开始划到湖中心去吧！划到更远的湖的深处去吧！远离人群吧！站起来吧！挑战高难度的动作吧……

当你偏离动作规范，即使微小的动作也能感受到桨板的不配合时，才会收起自己的傲慢，谦卑起来。

Tips

### 漂流

藏龙百瀑漂流位于天荒坪镇大溪村，是一条全长2.5千米的漂流河道，用时约2小时，水流相对平缓，适合亲子、情侣、闺蜜出游，打发无聊悠长的夏日时光。一个激流之后，如果划桨不当，有可能充分体验到“水不但能载舟，亦能覆舟，还能让舟原地打转”的惊险刺激。

### 瀑布

当你满头大汗站在倾泻而下的一面瀑布前，会忘了上山的苦。奔腾的气势，飞溅的水珠，沉默的水遇到沉默的山石，轰鸣入耳，这才是“沉默振聋发聩”。可以去藏龙百瀑，那里瀑布众多，一路往山上走，且走且遇见各种规模的瀑布。也可以去瀑布咖啡（巴厘岛版），这里的瀑布有三级，都气势宏大。

### 湖泊

In · 竹野躺平基地位于山川乡大里村桃坑水库，沿湖搭建了许多临水天幕，风景清幽可人。同样位于大里村的云下湖畔的水上项目有皮划艇、桨板、潜水，感受人与工具的合二为一，短暂的对于大自然的某种征服。

## Summer Invasion Plan!

The best summer retreat isn't a seaside town, a beach, or a sun umbrella. It's deep in the mountains, where you're given a lake, a waterfall, and a drifting experience. Here, you'll spend a summer that's rich and vibrant, yet peaceful and refreshing.

Du Yu Cun is home to many lakes, most of which are surrounded by mountains. The waters are tranquil and serene, and in the shadow of the green mountains, they stand defiant against the scorching sun. Each lake, like it's very essence, exudes an unfathomable charm. There are few "wild lakes" without owners here. No matter how silent they may be, the shores are always dotted with various activities and thrilling water sports that are developed around the lakes.

When we arrived at Xingchao Camp, a group of elementary school students was practicing paddleboarding by the lake. The young and handsome coach patiently demonstrated the proper paddleboarding techniques with both words and body language. Completely unfamiliar with paddleboarding, we obediently watched, just like students in class: forward, steady the paddle, reverse... kneeling, standing, half-standing...

After mastering the theoretical part, I still felt nervous as I got on the paddleboard. The lifeguard, casually standing by, reassured me, saying, "Falling into the water is normal." This was probably the worst thing he could have said — suddenly, my fear increased by threefold.

I couldn't help but glance at the safety leash on my ankle, and my mind began to imagine various scenarios of how I might escape if I fell into the water. Would the leash really help? What if I fell headfirst, with my feet in the air? How would I save myself?

Despite the fear, once I got on the paddleboard and combined theory with practice, I quickly got the hang of it. Forward, backward, steady the paddle! I had a great time.

The subtle interaction and balance between the person and the paddleboard, after repeated trials, made it easy to mistakenly believe that this was just a one-sided skill to master. This led to a sort of"man and paddleboard unity" arrogance: "Let's paddle from the shore to the center of the lake!" "Let's go further into the deep lake!" "Let's get away from the crowds!" "Stand up!" "Let's try more challenging moves..."

But when you deviate from the correct movements, even the smallest misstep will make you feel the paddleboard's resistance. It's only then that you set aside your arrogance and approach the experience with humility.

## Tips:

### Rafting

The rafting at Canglong Baipu Waterfalls is located in Daxi Village,

Tianhuangping Town. It is a rafting river with a total length of 2.5 kilometers, and it takes about 2 hours. The water flow is relatively gentle, making it suitable for parent-child outings, couples, and female friends to enjoy. It is a good way to kill the long and boring summer time. After a turbulent current, if you paddle improperly, you may fully experience the thrilling excitement of "water can not only carry a boat, but also capsize it, and even make the boat spin in place".

### Lake

The In· Bamboo Wild Relaxation Base is located in Dali Village, Shanchuan Township. At Taokeng Reservoir, many waterside canopies have been built along the lake, and the scenery is quiet and lovely. At the lakeside under the clouds in Dali Village, there are water activities such as kayaking, stand-up paddleboarding, and diving, allowing people to experience the integration of human beings and tools and have a short-term conquest of nature in a certain way.

### Waterfall

When you stand in front of a cascading waterfall, perspiring profusely, you will forget the hardship of climbing up the mountain. The surging momentum, the splashing water droplets, and the silent water meeting the silent rocks, with the rumbling sound reaching your ears, this is exactly what is meant by "silence being deafening". You can go to Canglong Baipu Waterfalls, where there are numerous waterfalls. As you walk up the mountain, you will encounter waterfalls of various scales along the way. You can also go to the Waterfall Coffee (Bali version), where there are three tiers of waterfalls, all of which are of great momentum.

# 此刻的秋 手可摘星辰

文 / 刘林

来大余村之前，我只在夏天拍过星星。彼时，在远离城市的喧嚣与强光的昏暗之中，架起三脚架，手动对焦，开启长曝光模式，放任相机自己工作。而后我与朋友抬头，那是我第一次看见了银河，也看见了课本上的北斗七星，以及体验了蚊虫袭来时，我疯狂拍打的狼狈。所以我记忆中的看星星，是如同夏日一般喧闹的梦境。

在大余村观星，却是另一种体验。

秋风开始轻拂大地，树叶染上五彩斑斓的颜色，大余村有了天然的静谧之美。秋天这个季节也很妙，此时的星空不再是夏夜那遥远而朦胧的梦境，也不是冬夜因寒冷而匆匆一瞥的璀璨，而是以一种恰到好处的姿态，呈现在每一位仰望者——包括我的面前。

“自古逢秋悲寂寥，我言秋日胜春朝。”我突然就懂了古人的言下之意。

## Tips

秋季温度适宜，晴朗天气较多，银河在星空的位置较高，更容易被观察到；一些著名的星座如仙后座、飞马座都很容易被找到。因此，秋季是观星的大好季节。2024 年，第二届安吉观星节在天荒坪瀑布咖啡·星空营地开启。

### 授人以鱼，大余村，在哪里观星？

景区，云上草原和江南天池因为海拔高，有多处优质观星点；村落，山川乡九亩村有“浙北高山第一村”之称，上墅乡龙王村、董岭村海拔也都较高，适宜观星；其他场所，如瀑布咖啡（星空版）、云上草原星空酒店等也有观星的条件。

## 授人以渔，如何寻找到满意的观星点？

尽量挑选远离灯光、视野开阔、海拔高的地方，避免有强光干扰的区域。提前查看天气预报，选择晴朗无云的夜晚。秋季观星的最佳时间通常在晚上 9 点至凌晨 2 点，此时天空较暗，星星更加明显。

## 观星，需要准备什么？

一台帮助你观察美的望远镜，
一台帮你记录美的相机，
一些辅助你寻找美的小道具，

最重要的是，一双善于发现美的眼睛，
用眼睛感受星空的美，就足够啦。

## *Autumn at This Moment: Hands That Can Pick the Stars*

Before coming to Da Yu Cun, I had only ever photographed stars in the summer. At that time, far from the city's noise and the dimming of the strong lights, I would set up a tripod, manually focus, and switch to long exposure mode, allowing the camera to do it's work. Then, with my friends, I would look up, and that was the first time I saw the Milky Way, the Big Dipper from our textbooks, and experienced the desperate swatting of mosquitoes in a frantic attempt to escape their attacks. So, in my memory, stargazing was like a noisy summer dream.

However, stargazing in Da Yu Cun was a completely different experience.

The autumn wind began to gently caress the earth, the leaves turning vibrant hues, and the village was imbued with a natural tranquility. Autumn is truly a wonderful season. The stars in the sky at this time no longer feel like the distant, hazy dreams of a summer night, nor the fleeting brilliance of a winter night, quickly glanced at in the cold. Instead, they are presented in just the right manner, visible to anyone who gazes up—myself included.

"Since ancient times, autumn has been a season of sadness and solitude, but I say autumn surpasses spring mornings." Suddenly, I understood the meaning behind the ancient words.

## Tips:

In autumn, the temperature is pleasant and there are more sunny days. The Milky Way is at a higher position in the sky, making it easier to observe. Some well - known constellations such as Cassiopeia and Pegasus are also easy to find. Therefore, autumn is an excellent season for stargazing. In 2024, the second Anji Stargazing Festival was held at Tianhuangping Waterfall Coffee • Starry Sky Camp.

**Where can we stargaze in Da Yu Cun?**

Due to their high altitudes, both Sky Land and the Jiangnan Tianchi have multiple high-quality stargazing spots. Jiumu Village in Shanchuan Township is known as the "First Alpine Village in Northern

Zhejiang", and both Longwang Village and Dongling Village in Shangshu Township also have relatively high altitudes, making them suitable for stargazing. Other places, such as Waterfall Coffee (Starry Sky Version) and the Starry Sky Hotel in the Grassland Above the Clouds, also have the conditions for stargazing.

### How to find a good stargazing spot?

Try to choose places that are far away from lights, have a wide field of vision, and are at a high altitude, and avoid areas with strong light interference. Check the weather forecast in advance and choose a clear and cloudless night. The best time for stargazing in autumn is usually between 9 pm and 2 am, during which the sky is darker and the stars are more noticeable.

### What to prepare?

A telescope that helps you observe beauty,
A camera that helps you record beauty,
Some small props that assist you in finding beauty,
Most importantly, a pair of eyes that are good at discovering beauty.
It's enough to feel the beauty of the starry sky with your eyes.

# 论在南方玩雪的积极心理学层面的意义

文 / 王偶得

这世上很多伟大的发现和创造有时基于偶然。

美国著名心理学家、美国心理学会"终身成就奖"获得者马丁·赛利格曼在创立积极心理学之前，一直沉浸其中、无法自拔、持续进行的却是对消极心理学的研究，以致他在此过程中也受到阴郁、负面情绪的浸染，差点让自己成为被研究对象。偶然一次和5岁女儿的对话，令他对自己的状态幡然醒悟："爸爸，如果我不再抱怨了，你也可以不再经常郁闷吗？"于是，一段日常生活的对话催生了"积极心理学之父"。

积极心理学跟在南方玩雪有什么关系呢？当"南方"和"雪"两个词摆在一起时，就等同于稀有，而后就是不可错过，这就令身体开始大量分泌多巴胺，促使我们发现哪里有雪、怎么观赏、怎么玩，产生一系列渴望。比如我们选择了去云上草原和江南天池滑雪，同样是高海拔的滑雪场却拥有不同的景致，于是就有了各自的期待。在这个过程中，出发之前会想象高海拔之上的雪景，再想象滑雪时速度、温度，以及风给我们带来的不同层面的感受。等真正开始滑雪时，那种只有在现场、只有自己才能体会的激情和愉悦给我们带来了足够的快乐与满足。这也是人类区别于动物的特质之一——人类大脑前额叶的参与让我们理解和判断此时此刻、此情此景所感就是幸福。

不过话分两头。陀翁说过："爱生活，不爱生活的意义。"下雪时，去玩就是了，想那么多干吗呢，费神！

## Tips

大余村冬天赏雪、玩雪都要往高海拔的地方走。赏雪可以去山川乡的中国金钱松森林公园，在海拔900米之上，见过了一眼万年的金钱松秋韵，再来赏一场可以媲美长白山冬雪的雪景，或许一愣神的工夫你就忘记自己身处安吉。

对于想要、喜欢滑雪的人，推荐云上草原、江南天池和观音堂这三处滑雪场。

### 云上草原滑雪场

南方最大的滑雪场，硬件设施最强。

雪场面积：30万平方米。

专业雪道：2条高级道+3条中级道+2条初级道，雪道总长3.8千米，最长雪道1000米。

雪具大厅：1.1万平方米，设施齐全。

专业加持：500多名来自体育学院的专业滑雪教练。

雪场运力：双人+四人吊椅式缆车、11条魔毯。

花式娱雪：2.2万平方米嬉雪乐园，
10多家高山户外雪游乐园。

雾凇仙境：360°全景沉浸式观雪体验。

停车场选择：云上草原国际山地旅游度假区游客中心停车场、2号停车场、北弄停车场。

购票&入园：网上购票的客人须至游客中心购买索道票后入园，或直接至游客中心购买门票+索道票。

注：索道是进出云上草原景区的唯一方式。

✉ 山川乡高家堂村

## 江南天池滑雪场

一半清冷，一半温情。

雪场面积：6 万平方米。

长度：近 800 米。

落差：40 米。

专业雪道：高级滑雪道、中级滑雪道、初级滑雪道和儿童雪圈道及戏雪场。

高山汤泉：4 万平方米。

泡池：室内 15 个，室外 28 个。

✉ 天荒坪镇

## 观音堂滑雪场

坡度较缓，亲子首选。

雪场面积：1.4 万平方米。

缓坡雪道：2 条近 300 米雪道 +3 条近 200 米雪道。

亲子嬉雪区：近 1 万平方米。

泡池：室内 15 个，室外 28 个。

✉ 天荒坪上水库

# *On the Positive Psychological Significance of Playing in the Snow in the South*

Many great discoveries and creations in this world sometimes stem from chance.

Before founding positive psychology, the renowned American psychologist and recipient of the American Psychological Association's Lifetime Achievement Award, Martin Seligman, was deeply immersed in and almost consumed by the study of negative psychology. His constant focus on negative emotions nearly led him to become the subject of his own research. One day, a casual conversation with his 5-year-old daughter made him realize his own state: "Dad, if I stop complaining, can you stop being so gloomy too?" This simple exchange sparked the birth of positive psychology, earning him the title "Father of Positive Psychology."

What does positive psychology have to do with playing in the snow in the South? When the words "South" and "snow" are put together, they become synonymous with rarity, which immediately triggers a flood of dopamine in the brain. This neurotransmitter compels us to seek out snow, figure out how to enjoy it, and indulge in various desires. For instance, we choose to go skiing at places like Sky Land and Jiangnan Tianchi. Both are high-altitude ski resorts, yet each offers a unique landscape, creating different sets of expectations. In this process, before we even depart, we imagine the snowy vistas at high altitudes, then imagine the speed, temperature, and the sensations brought on by the wind during skiing. When we finally ski, the unique thrill and joy only experienced firsthand provide us with enough happiness and satisfaction. This is one of the qualities that set humans apart from animals—the involvement of the prefrontal cortex in the human brain helps us understand and judge that the happiness we feel in the moment is genuine.

However, as Tolstoy once said, "Love life, not the meaning of life." When it snows, just go out and play—why overthink it? It's a waste of energy!

## Tips:

In winter, if you want to enjoy and play with the snow in Dayu Village, you need to go to places with high altitudes. For snow viewing, you can go to the Golden Larch Forest Park in Shanchuan Township, which is located at an altitude of over 900 meters. After experiencing the autumn charm of the Golden Larch that seems to have remained unchanged for thousands of years, coming here to admire a snow scene that can rival the winter snow in Changbai Mountain, perhaps in a blink of an eye, you will forget that you are in Anji.

For those who want to ski or are fond of skiing, three ski resorts are **recommended:** Yunshang Prairie, Jiangnan Tianchi, and Guanyintang.

**Skyland Ski Resort**

It is the largest ski resort in the south of China with the most powerful hardware facilities.

**Ski Resort Area:** 300,000 square meters.

**Professional Ski Runs:** 2 advanced runs + 3 intermediate runs + 2 beginner runs. The total length of the ski runs is 3.8 kilometers, and the longest ski run is 1,000 meters.

**Ski Equipment Hall:** With an area of 11,000 square meters, it is fully equipped.

**Professional Support:** More than 500 professional skiing coaches from sports academies.

**Ski Resort Transportation Capacity:** Double-person and four-person chairlifts, and 11 magic carpets.

**Diversified Snow Entertainment:** A 22,000-square-meter snow-playing paradise and more than 10 alpine outdoor snow amusement parks.

**Rime Wonderland:** A 360° panoramic immersive snow-viewing experience.

**Parking Lot Options:** The Parking Lot of Skyland International

Mountain Tourism Resort Visitor Center, Parking Lot No. 2, and Beinong Parking Lot.

**Ticket Purchase & Entrance:** Guests who purchase tickets online must go to the visitor center to buy cable car tickets before entering the park, or directly go to the visitor center to buy entrance tickets + cable car tickets.

**Note:** The cable car is the only way to enter and exit the Skyland Scenic Area.

**Address:** Gaojiatang Village, Shanchuan Township

**Jiangnan Tianchi Ski Resort**

It is both a bit chilly and a bit warm.

**Ski Resort Area:** 60,000 square meters.

**Length:** Nearly 800 meters.

**Drop:** 40 meters.

**Professional Ski Runs:** Advanced ski runs, intermediate ski runs, beginner ski runs, a children's snow tube lane and a snow-playing area.

**Alpine Hot Spring:** Covering an area of 40000 square meters.

**Hot Spring Pools:** 15 indoor ones and 28 outdoor ones.

**Address:** Tianhuangping Town

**Guanyintang Ski Resort**

It has a gentle slope, making it the first choice for parent-child activities.

**Ski Resort Area:** 14,000 square meters.

**Gentle Slope Ski Runs:** 2 ski runs of nearly 300 meters + 3 ski runs of nearly 200 meters.

**Parent-child Snow-playing Area:** Nearly 10,000 square meters.

**Hot Spring Pools:** 15 indoor ones and 28 outdoor ones.

**Address:** The Upper Reservoir in Tianhuangping Town

# 饮居岁月

Accommodation and meals

# 山野里的美味有它自己的智慧

文 / 刘林

在大余村的山野里寻到美味，是一件简单却又困难的事。

说简单，无非源于山野之间，一草一木旁，一溪一湖间，处处是大自然的馈赠。

春日里，肆意生长的野菜隐匿于田野的缝隙间，高山上的茶叶也以勃勃生机展示着独特的清香；夏日里，溯溪畅游的石斑鱼、跻身石缝中的小虾，鲜美无比，只须简单烹饪，便能让人回味无穷；秋风起时，林间果实累累，山核桃、板栗、柿子……自然成熟的甘甜，是大自然对勤劳者的奖赏；冬日虽寒，却也有深藏不露的野味，冬笋在皑皑白雪下静静生长，等待着有心人的挖掘。

说困难，则是想要它们从山野之间来到餐桌之上，人们总要和自然的智慧进行角逐。

寻野菜，眼神要好，知识也要掌握得牢，往往年轻人还没分清野草和野菜的区别在哪里，老人家已经三两下将一筐野菜摘下。采茶，山高路远，只能人工采。采茶人背负着竹篓，手持竹篮，穿梭在茶树间，手指在嫩绿的叶芽间跳跃，可谓“叶叶皆辛苦”。

石斑鱼喜欢在水草区、洄水湾、树荫下等地方活动，也只在晴朗、温暖的

天气下活跃度较高，才更容易上钩。若想吃上新鲜的石斑鱼，还得选好地方和天气。

山核桃要看准节气，白露一到，便意味着山核桃成熟了。打山核桃是一项体力活，要举着十几米长的竹竿往树上抽，一下一下将山核桃打落在地；也是一项技术活，要瞄准，掌握好挥竿的力度和角度，否则极有可能打了空竿，白白浪费了力气。

至于挖笋，也有一些讲究。对于春笋而言，最佳挖掘时节为每年三月中下旬至清明前后，此时春笋最为鲜嫩。冬笋挖掘的时机更为微妙，需要寻找的是尚未露头的冬笋，一旦冒出地面，其口感和品质就会大打折扣。

看来，探寻山野之味的核心要义，便在于如何以一种和谐共生的态度与自然亲密对话。

Tips

## 准备妥当，在哪里可以吃到山珍？

竹笋 & 野菜：春日里来天荒坪、上墅、山川的任意村落，都可以品尝到这些美味。要想吃得与众不同一些，可以去天荒坪探索“百笋宴”；多数民宿、农家乐应季地会有带客人一同挖野菜、挖竹笋的活动。

山核桃：天荒坪镇大溪村、上墅乡董岭村是山核桃的量产地。白露节气一过，去往这两个村落里总能找到“新鲜出炉”的山核桃。一个冷知识：黑色的山核桃是水煮的，木色的山核桃是炒的。前者吃起来更不容易上火。

石斑鱼：山川乡的石斑鱼最为有名，在当地被称为“山溪小精灵”，一般的农家乐餐厅都有售卖；当然啦，昂刺鱼、小杂鱼也是不错的选择。

高山云雾茶：安吉白茶固然不可错过，但上墅乡董岭村的高山云雾茶，无论是绿茶还是红茶，都别有一番风味。

## *The Delights of the Wild Have Their Own Wisdom*

Finding delicious food in the mountains and fields of Da Yu Cun is a simple yet challenging task.

It is simple because, in the fields and mountains, by every plant, tree, stream, and lake, nature offers it's bounty.

In spring, wild vegetables grow freely in the cracks of the fields, and the tea leaves on the high mountains exude a unique fragrance with vibrant life; in summer, the stone bass swimming up the streams and the small shrimp hidden in the crevices of rocks are incredibly fresh—requiring only simple cooking to leave a lasting aftertaste; when the autumn breeze arrives, the forest is full of fruit's—Chinese walnuts, chestnuts, persimmons... the naturally ripened sweetness is nature's reward for the diligent; though winter is cold, it hides wild delicacies too, like the winter bamboo shoots that quietly grow under the thick snow, waiting to be discovered.

The challenge lies in bringing these treasures from the wild to the table — one must compete with nature's wisdom.

To find wild vegetables, one must have sharp eyes and solid knowledge. While young people often can't distinguish between wild grass and wild vegetables, the elders can gather a basket of them in no time. Picking tea leaves involves trekking high, rugged paths, as it can only be done by hand. Tea pickers carry bamboo baskets, moving through the tea trees, their fingers jumping between the tender green leaves—every leaf is harvested with care and effort.

Grouper prefers to stay in areas with water plants, eddies, and shade, and is only active on clear, warm days, making it more likely to bite when conditions are right.

Chinese walnuts ripen with the white dew in the air, and picking them is hard work. A long bamboo pole must be used to strike the tree, knocking the walnuts to the ground, requiring both strength and skill. If the aim or technique is off, one might strike air and waste energy.

When digging for bamboo shoots, timing is crucial. Spring bamboo shoots are best harvested from mid to late March, just before Qingming, when they are at their freshest. Winter bamboo shoots require even more attention. They must be harvested before they emerge from the ground, as their taste and quality diminish once they surface.

It seems the key to discovering the flavors of the wild lies in how one engages with nature in a harmonious, symbiotic way.

## *Tips:*

The person is ready, so where can these delicacies be enjoyed?

**Bamboo Shoots & Wild Vegetables:** In the springtime, you can savor these delicacies in any village in Tianhuangping, Shangshu, or Shanchuan. For a unique dining experience, explore the "Hundred Bamboo Shoots Feast" in Tianhuangping.

**Chinese Walnut:** Daxi Village in Tianhuangping and Dongling Village in Shangshu are well-known for their abundant production of Chinese walnuts.

**Grouper:** The Grouper from Shanchuan Township is particularly famous and is locally known as the "little fairy of mountain streams." It is commonly available in most agritainment restaurants.

**High-Mountain Cloud and Mist Tea:** While Anji White Tea is certainly not to be missed, the high-mountain cloud and mist tea from Dongling Village in Shangshu, whether green tea or black tea, offers a unique flavor.

文 / 樊多多

# 真香定律之大余村实验

色与视觉相关，香与嗅觉亲近，它们一起构成打开味蕾和胃口第一道防线的同盟军。正餐也好，小吃也罢，又或者咖啡、酒水、下午茶，没有色、香开道，都轮不到滋味出场。

在余村逛吃逛吃，我总是犯病——选择困难症日渐严重，于是放弃选择，开启“我都要”模式。

第一天，我去考察了青来食堂。原本以为这里该是 DN 余村数字游民的吃饭大本营，不承想与好几桌外地游客在此互通有无。他们已在此晃荡了 3 天，去了人多玩法多的云上草原，也到了井空里大峡谷探了险，于是问我哪里有小众、安静、适合慢慢荡的好去处。我仔细搜索还不太熟悉的大余村，于是给他们指了一条明路——住在小余村，晚饭后、可以在村子里走余村邮局 — 乡音小馆 — 青年图书馆的小环线，也可以沿着镇中路以 City Walk 的方式往银坑村方向慢慢行去……就着饭聊天，大家在青来食堂就这么随意吃下去了两碗饭。

经过连续几餐对青来食堂的考察，我决定换换口味，到余村食堂去探寻一番，它还有个很文艺的名字——长歌行餐厅。本来是冲着他们家的沸腾鱼而来，却被店内的小甜筒斩获芳心。依然是偏题的一餐，心里暗暗许愿：下次一定来体验一下户外平台上的浪漫晚餐。

随后几天，我涉猎的范围逐渐扩大，按时段涵盖早、中、晚餐，按类型囊括农家菜、面馆、烧烤等，不一而足，如叶家烧饼加上吴均汤包的混合式早餐，习风堂文化主题餐厅的精致料理，春林山庄农家菜的舌尖乡愁，天荒坪

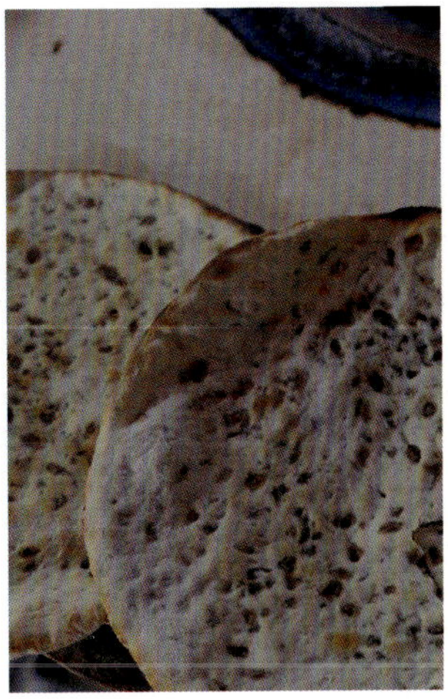

烧烤一条街的人间烟火味，就连当地的特产风物如冬笋、山核桃、香榧等也悉数收入胃中，重点体现杂和精。

经过几天的一线考察，从吃这件事上认知余村，我得出如下结论：除去用餐的氛围感光环，新鲜的食材和高超的烹饪技艺是大余村美食的真香定律！

## Tips

初来大余村，从“吃”入手能很快进入“在这里”的生活状态。以镇中路为中心，呈网状四散开去。在天荒坪镇可以选择青来食堂、长歌行、YuLi 余里·花园餐厅、习风堂文化主题餐厅、叶家烧饼、吴均汤包非遗美食等，在山川乡可以选择竹里农家菜、稻禧饭堂、子妍面馆等，在上墅乡可以选择硒食餐厅、青石上民宿餐厅等，玩味余村，一日三餐，一网打尽。

## *The Law of "Smells Good" — The Da Yu Cun Experiment*

Colors relate to vision, while smells are linked to the sense of taste. Together, they form an alliance that opens the first line of defense for our taste buds and appetite. Whether it's a full meal, a snack, coffee, alcohol, or afternoon tea, without the allure of color and fragrance, taste will never have its turn.

While wandering around Yucun Village, I always face a dilemma—my choice paralysis becomes increasingly severe. So, I abandon the act of choosing and switch to the "I want everything" mode.

On the first day, I visited Qinglai Canteen. I originally thought it would be the main dining spot for the digital nomads in Yucun Village, but it turned out to be a gathering place for several tables of out-of-town tourists. They had been in the area for three days, visiting the popular and fun Skyland, and exploring the scenic Jinkongli Grand Canyon. They asked me where there were quiet, off-the-beaten-path spots for a relaxing time. I racked my brain, searching for places in Da Yu Cun that I wasn't yet familiar with, and then gave them a solid suggestion: stay in Yucun village, and after dinner, take a leisurely walk around the village, passing by the Yucun Post Office, Xiangyin Tavern, and the Youth Library, or take a city walk along Zhenzhong Road toward Yinkeng Village. While chatting over dinner, we casually had two bowls of rice at Qinglai Canteen.

After several visit's to Qinglai Canteen, I decided to try something new and headed to Dayu Canteen, which has a poetic name—Changge Xing Restaurant. I originally went there for their signature boiling fish, but ended up falling in love with their little icecream cones. It was another one of those off-topic meals, and I silently promised myself: next time, I'll come back for a romantic dinner on the outdoor platform.

In the following days, my culinary exploration gradually expanded. I covered breakfast, lunch and dinner, from farmhouse dishes, noodle shops to barbecues. I had a mixed breakfast of Ye's baked flatbread and Wu Jun's soup dumplings, delicate dishes at Xifengtang Cultural Theme Restaurant, the nostalgic taste of rural life at Chunlin Mountain Villa, and the smoky flavor of street barbecues at Tianhuangping Barbecue Street. Even local specialties like winter bamboo shoots, Chinese walnuts, and fragrant torreya nuts found their way into my stomach, reflecting both variety and refinement.

After several days of hands-on exploration, I came to the conclusion about Yucun Village through the act of eating: aside from the ambiance of the dining experience, fresh ingredients and excellent cooking skills once again proved the truth of a delicious meal—the law of "smells good" is real, as Yi Yin's wisdom was not mistaken!

## Tips:

When you first come to Dayu Village, starting with "eating" can quickly help you get into the local life state. Centered around Zhenzhong Road, various dining options spread out in a network. In Tianhuangping Town, you can choose Qinglai Canteen, Changgexing, YuLi · Garden Restaurant, Xifengtang Cultural Theme Restaurant, Ye's Sesame Seed Cakes, Wujun's Soup Dumplings (an intangible cultural heritage delicacy), etc. In Shanchuan Township, you can choose Zhuli Farmhouse Cuisine, Daoxi Canteen, Ziyan Noodle Restaurant, etc. In Shangshu Township, you can choose Xishí Restaurant, Qingshishang Homestay Restaurant, etc. Enjoy the food in Yucun Village and cover all three meals a day.

# 梦回
# 州桥夜市

文 / 安然

入夜，走在安吉“青来集”的烧烤一条街上，这里露天摆满了桌椅，店小二都站在店外，热情地招揽顾客，有已经入座的客人，正自己动手开始烧烤，香气和烟雾缓慢地弥散开来，仿佛比赛一般，看谁先吸引路过的人群。很显然香气完全胜出，我们一行很快就抵挡不住这诱人的肉香酒香，挑选落座，开始了胡吃海喝的消夜生活。

翻阅史册会发现，北宋是中国古代少有的宵禁制度宽松的朝代，汴京御街“夜市直至三更尽，才五更又复开张”茶坊酒肆鳞次栉比，瓦肆勾栏彻夜喧腾。北宋的夜市虽盛，终究是坊市制度下的限定场景，而现代的消夜，却是全民的大舞台。尤其是天荒坪的烧烤别具一格，是云南特色，这与天荒坪抽水蓄能电站的建设者中有大批来自云南的工人有关。

所谓云南特色，即半米高的方桌上，中央开了一个方孔，下方稳稳地安置着一个铸铁炭盆。点燃炭火后，炭盆上方覆盖着一层钢丝网，只须将精选的食材直接铺在网上，两面均匀烧烤即可。烤熟的食物还不能直接入口，而是要蘸上店家精心调配的灵魂蘸水——或酸辣，或咸香。任何食材，在蘸水的包裹下，都仿佛被赋予了新的生命，回味无穷。

露天烧烤、啤酒、邻桌的欢声笑语、彼此缠夹不清的肉的香味、旁边的河流、站在一旁安静的树、树上的霓虹灯，还有星辰、微风……这一切自然与烟火气息缠绕应和，使我们不自觉地丢弃种种餐桌礼仪，豪放地喝酒吃肉、大声讲话，杯子是不需要的，吹瓶即可。

消夜的盛行，未必是对健康饮食的舍弃，而是一种生活态度和自由的选择。自律是一种健康，有所节制的放纵也是一种健康。若是《东京梦华录》里的汴京百姓穿越至今，或许也会惊叹于这无边夜色中的盛宴——在这个时空维度被打破的夜晚，从州桥夜市到天荒坪烧烤，人们对于夜色美好的追求从未改变。

## Tips

烧烤场往往由黄昏起直到深夜。可以自己烤，也可以让店家帮你烤好拿过来。桌椅沿河而设，烟火气息和大自然浑然一体，有时候你会有一种错觉，仿佛你是一个抛弃了现代文明的古人，刚学会钻木取火，对于熟食有一种极致的渴望，迫不及待地想大快朵颐。有时化身绿林大侠，粗野豪放。

⊠ “青来集”烧烤一条街；或是干脆去天荒坪镇上闲逛，大概率能遇到一些令人惊喜的烧烤店。

✳ 余村的数字游民们经过半年的调研和编辑，编写了一本《天荒坪云南烧烤完全指南》，可以关注他们的公众号“DNCN”了解更多天荒坪烧烤的故事。

## Dreaming Back to the Zhouqiao Night Market

As night falls, walking through the barbecue street at Anji's "Qinglai Ji" ,the open-air space is filled with tables and chairs. The shopkeepers stand outside, eagerly calling in customers. Some diners have already sat down, starting their own grilling, and the aroma and smoke slowly spread through the air, as if in a competition to see who can attract the most passersby. Clearly, the aroma wins. Our group quickly succumbs to the tempting smells of grilled meat and alcohol, choosing a spot to settle in and start our late-night feast.

Flipping through historical records, one discovers that the Northern Song Dynasty was one of the few ancient Chinese dynasties with relaxed curfew policies. The imperial streets of Bianjing (modern-day Kaifeng) saw night markets that "lasted until the third watch (midnight), only to reopen at the fifth watch (before dawn)." Teahouses and taverns lined the streets, while entertainment venues buzzed with activity all night long. Though the night markets of the Northern Song were vibrant, they were still confined within the rigid urban ward system. In contrast, modern-night snacking is a grand stage for all. Particularly unique are Tianhuangping's barbecue stalls, which carry a distinct Yunnan flavor—a legacy of the many Yunnan workers who built the Tianhuangping Pumped Storage Power Station.

The Yunnan flavor refers to the setup of a half-meter-high square table, with a square hole in the center, below which is placed a sturdy cast-iron charcoal basket. After the charcoal is lit, a steel wire mesh covers the top. You simply place the selected ingredients directly on the mesh and grill them evenly on both sides. But the grilled food cannot be eaten immediately. Instead, it must be dipped in the restaurant's carefully crafted soul sauce—either spicy and sour, or salty and fragrant. Any ingredient, wrapped in this sauce, seems to be infused with new life, leaving a lingering aftertaste.

Outdoor barbecues, beer, the laughter of the neighboring table, the mingling aroma of tangled meat, the nearby river, the quiet trees standing by, neon lights in the branches, along with the stars and a gentle breeze... all of these elements naturally blend with the lively, smoky atmosphere. They make us unconsciously forget about table manners, drinking and eating meat boldly, speaking loudly, with no need for glasses – just a bottle to blow from.

The popularity of late-night snacks does not necessarily mean abandoning healthy eating habits, but rather reflects a lifestyle and a choice of freedom. Discipline is a form of health, and measured indulgence is another. If the people of Bianjing from A Dream of Splendor could time-travel to today, they might marvel at this boundless nocturnal feast—where the pursuit of nightlife's pleasures remains unchanged, from the Zhouqiao Night Market to Tianhuangping's barbecue, across the unbroken span of time.

## Tips:

The barbecue places are usually bustling from dusk until late night, as lively as a ghost market. You can grill the food yourself, or ask the store owner to grill it and bring it to you. The tables and chairs are set up along the river, and the hustle and bustle of the barbecue blends seamlessly with nature. Sometimes, you may have an illusion that you are an ancient person who has abandoned modern civilization, having just learned how to make a fire by rubbing wood together, with an intense craving for cooked food and eagerly devouring it. At other times, you might feel like a heroic figure in the greenwood, rough and unrestrained.

**Address:** Qinglaiji Barbecue Street; or simply stroll around Tianhuangping Town, where you're likely to stumble upon some delightful barbecue shops.

* The digital nomads of Da Yu Cun have compiled a "Complete Guide to Yunnan-style Barbecue in Tianhuangping." For more stories about Tianhuangping's barbecue, follow their official account "DNCN".

# 爱与自由

文／樊多多

“我活在世上，无非想要明白些道理，遇见些有趣的事。倘能如我愿，我的一生就算成功。”

手里拿着《红拂夜奔》，嘴里念叨着我最喜欢的王小波语录，回忆着刚刚结束的特种兵式民宿打卡年假，不由觉得自己也是走在成功之路上的践行者。毕竟这些天住的那些民宿每一家都称得上有趣，甚至脑洞大开、天马行空。他们在“住”这件事上挖空心思，身体力行，想要做到极致，无非也是想要明白一些生活的道理，遇到一些有趣的人来一起分享罢了。红拂女选择在漆黑之夜奔赴李靖，我选择用 7 天时间体验大余村的五家民宿，形式不同、目的对象不同，但初衷一致，本质上无他：都是为了爱与自由，像风一样，如梦一般，生动而鲜活。

Tips

**I 大余村有哪些有趣的民宿？**

### 原力山谷

直指宇宙奥秘的体验之旅，形似白兵头盔的建筑外形随意散落在山谷，那里就是旅人的栖息地；蓝色星球造型的滑滑梯、攀爬架，吸引着我们进入这个《星球大战》主题的科幻世界。

适宜人群：亲子、情侣和团建。
玩法体验：楼顶烧烤露营、露天影院、天文望远、星空泡泡屋、竹林挖笋、溪边翻蟹。
✉ 上墅乡龙王村杨家岭 4 号

### 松果民宿

你到山中来，生活在别处，却依然可以像在自己家一样自由。用 30 年以上树龄的松木打造的窗框和家具，带着大自然的原始气息。风车茉莉花开的时候来到松果民宿，满墙花树足以慰风尘。

特色美食：西餐、烧烤、特色农家菜。
✉ 上墅乡上墅村下四房自然村 40 号

## 艾伦家

如果你爱宫崎骏，你将在艾伦家遇见《天空之城》《风之谷》《龙猫》，你可以选择住到贴着自己喜欢的电影海报的房间去，那里面有着和海报主题一样的整体色调，沉浸其中，无法自拔。你也可以让民宿主人的儿子小艾伦，带领你参观、入住，这里是妈妈为他打造的家，也是你的家。

适宜人群：亲子、情侣。
特色美食：牛肉丝锅仔、鱼头豆腐锅。
玩法体验：喝咖啡、溪里抓鱼等。
✉ 上墅乡施阮村 51 号

## 云竹谷

一位奶奶为自己的孙女打造的云朵主题梦幻城堡，这个童真沉浸式体验场欢迎所有大小朋友，被云朵包裹，被温柔以待。

适宜人群：亲子游。
玩法体验：云朵形的游泳池、六角形的蜂巢房间，彩色旋转楼梯是进入民宿的秘密通道。
特色美食：高山有机蔬菜和古法养殖的土鸡等安吉美食。
✉ 上墅乡龙王村过路滩自然村 43 号

## 璞拉那

以梵语 Prana 来命名民宿，确切地说这是一家有着民宿内涵、精品酒店装备的复合式住宿空间，可见民宿主理人对于旅人在璞拉那入住的期许——自由地呼吸，回归生命能量。而在这种静谧又放松的环境里，你吃早餐时，可能酒店总经理就坐在你旁边聆听你对住宿体验的满意度调查；如果你想去跑山，也会有人为你规划适合的路线。总之在璞拉那，除了享受齐全的设备、丰富的美食，还有很多不期而遇的喜悦。

适宜人群：家庭、亲子、情侣。
特色美食：全日制餐厅、中餐包厢、露天烧烤池等任君选择，竹笋、竹林鸡、小溪鱼等山间珍馐任君品尝。
玩法体验：去酒店专属的蔬菜农场体验采摘，周边还有日咖夜酒、瀑布咖啡、云下湖畔等休闲空间可以游玩。
✉ 山川乡船村自然村 188 号

## *Love and Freedom*

"I live in this world for no other reason than to understand some truths and encounter some interesting things. If I can achieve this, my life will be a success."

Holding Red Dust Rebellion at Midnight in my hands, I recite my favorite quote from Wang Xiaobo, reminiscing about my just-concluded, special-forces-style vacation of hopping between boutique homestays. I can't help but feel like a practitioner on the path to success. After all, every homestay I stayed in these past few days was fascinating—some even wildly imaginative and unconventional. These hosts have poured their hearts into the concept of "living," striving for the ultimate experience. And in doing so, they simply wish to grasp a few truths about life and meet some interesting people to share it with. Just as Lady Hongfu fled into the night to seek out Li Jing, I spent seven days staying in five homestays in Da Yu Cun. Different in form and purpose, yet identical in spirit—at it's core, it is all about love and freedom, like the wind, like a dream, vivid and alive.

## *Tips:*

What are the interesting homestays in Da Yu Cun?

- **Force Valley**

Experience a journey to the universe with Stormtrooper-helmet-like buildings and Star Wars-themed slides/climbing frames. Suitable for families, couples, and team-building. Activities include rooftop BBQ, outdoor cinema, star gazing, etc.

**Address:** No. 4, Yangjialing, Longwang Village, Shangshu Township

- **Pinecone Homestay**

Stay in a pine-crafted home surrounded by nature. Enjoy the blooming jasmine and relax. Specialties include Western cuisine, barbecue, and farm-style dishes.

**Address:** No. 40, Xiasifang Natural Village, Shangshu Village, Shangshu Township

• **Allen's Home**

Immerse yourself in Miyazaki-themed rooms at Allen's Home. Enjoy beef shred pot, fish head & tofu hot pot, coffee, and stream fishing. Suitable for families and couples.

**Address:** No. 51, Shiruan Village, Shangshu Township

• **Yunzhugu (Cloud Bamboo Valley)**

A grandmother built this dreamy cloud-themed castle for her granddaughter. This childlike immersive experience welcomes all friends, big and small, to be enveloped by clouds and treated with gentleness.

**Address:** No. 43, Guolutan Natural Village, Longwang Village, Shangshu Township

• **Prana**

Prana is a Sanskrit-named composite accommodation with homestay essence and boutique hotel equipment. Relax and rejuvenate in a peaceful environment. Enjoy mountain delicacies, picking at the hotel's farm, and exploring nearby spaces. Suitable for families and couples.

**Address:** No. 188, Chuancun Natural Village, Shanchuan Township

# 不可居无竹、无山、无水

文 / 刘林

苏轼曾经有云：“宁可食无肉，不可居无竹。无肉令人瘦，无竹令人俗。”可见，对于古人而言，住得风雅也是一种讲究。但要我说，在大余村，不可居无竹，也不可居无山、无水。

竹，是坚韧的赞歌，是自然之超凡脱俗的象征。竹之韵，在于其形。修长而挺拔的竹竿，宛如谦谦君子，无论雨打风吹，还是雪压霜欺，它都能保持那份独有的坚韧与傲骨。与竹居，是追求内心不卑不亢的生活哲学。

山，是大地的脊梁，自然之雄浑与壮阔的展现。群山环抱，层峦叠嶂，不仅提供了坚实的庇护，更让居住其中的人得以每日仰望那云雾缭绕的山巅，感受“会当凌绝顶，一览众山小”的豪迈。与山居，是在沉稳与深邃中，回归内心的豁达与纯粹。

水，是生命的源泉，自然之灵动的化身。或是见溪流潺潺，清泉石上流，或是看湖泊如镜，倒映着蓝天白云与周围的山色。水以其特有的温柔与包容，滋养了这片土地。与水居，是在繁忙与喧嚣之外，寻找一片属于自己的宁静港湾。

大余村境内的民宿，多与竹、山、水相伴，既是对古人“不可居无竹”的延续，也是对这份雅致更为全面的诠释与升华。

Tips

## 古道缘

古道缘是江南山居与现代美学的完美结合，外墙是中国传统夯土结构，内在保留了大量的原木结构，同时又有外挑阳台和大面积的落地窗，整体古朴而又自然，与山林相互呼应，却又能跳出环境令人眼前一亮。从屋后的古道一路走去便能找到白茶起源——白茶祖：一棵达百年树龄的野生茶树。

玩法体验：在古道缘，不仅可以爬古道寻白茶祖，还可以去大溪村村口的漂流，以及周边的九龙峡景区、江南天池游玩。

✉ 天荒坪镇大溪村横坑坞自然村

## 安吉开臣·息心庐

息心庐坐落于群山之间，竹林深处，环境幽静，融合了传统江南风味与现代简约风格，白墙、青瓦、重檐，与自然环境相得益彰。客房的建筑结构由中国美院的设计师精心设计，保留了原有的夯土墙结构，探索了更多老式风格与建筑学、美学等方面的融合与搭配。

玩法体验：民宿提供原生态的新鲜食材，落地大窗使窗外风景一览无余，可以在品尝美食的同时，欣赏窗外的美景，享受时光的美好。

✉ 天荒坪镇横路村横园里自然村 122 号

## 隐川居

隐川居的诞生，源于主人的一场日本之旅。他入住的日式民宿不仅环境雅致，更是远眺富士山美景的绝佳位置。当时主人心里的想法却是自己家乡的村庄就是依山而建，哪里比这里差？于是三年后，在山川乡多了一家名为“隐川居”的民宿，也多了一个供游人驻留欣赏安吉山水的好去处。

玩法体验：隐川居民宿周边自然风光优美，可以俯瞰峡谷群山，也可在井空里大峡谷溯溪、在高山上骑行。

✉ 山川乡船村村柘石岭

## 七间房·山川乡居

七间房装修风格简约而不失温馨，所有窗户均朝南，面向竹海。在这里，可以漫步山间小道，聆听鸟语虫鸣，感受大自然的宁静与和谐；也可以坐在民宿的露台或庭院中，品一杯香茗。建筑后面的山坡上有一棵据说是安吉县最大的红豆杉树，记得抽空去看一看。

玩法体验：露台观景、茶室品茗；附近有中国大竹海、安吉仙龙峡漂流、安吉灵溪山风景区等。

✉ 山川乡马家弄村梅石头自然村

## 云中溪·汤泉度假酒店

云中溪位于山谷之中，被郁郁葱葱的竹林和清澈的溪流环绕。酒店有23间客房，全部面向竹海开了落地窗。汤泉是这里的一大亮点，温泉水清澈透明，有多个特色汤池，如草药汤池、花香汤池等，供客人根据个人喜好选择。

玩法体验：270° 景观套房，有双层泳池、影音设施、户外篝火烧烤等；附近有江南天池、浙北大峡谷等景区。

✉ 上墅乡龙王村独山寺

## *A Residence Must Have Bamboo, Mountains, and Water*

Su Shi once said, "Better to live without meat than without bamboo. Without meat, one grows thin; without bamboo, one grows vulgar." To the ancients, a refined dwelling was a matter of principle. But in my opinion, in Da Yu Cun, a home must not only have bamboo but also mountains and water. Bamboo is an ode to resilience, a symbol of nature's transcendence.

The charm of bamboo lies in it's form—tall and straight, like a gentleman of integrity. Be it battered by wind and rain or weighed down by frost and snow, it retains it's unique resilience and dignity.

To live among bamboo is to pursue a life of balance and quiet strength.

Mountains are the backbone of the earth, a testament to nature's grandeur. Surrounded by towering peaks, crisscrossing ridges, and mist-shrouded summit's, one finds both shelter and inspiration. To gaze upon these mountains every day is to feel the boundless ambition of "Scaling the heights to view all beneath." To live among mountains is to embrace steadfastness and inner peace.

Water is the source of life, the embodiment of nature's fluid grace. Whether a murmuring stream flowing over stones or a lake still as a mirror, reflecting the sky and the mountains, water nourishes all it touches. To live by water is to find a personal refuge of serenity amid the noise of the world.

The homestays in Da Yu Cun are often nestled among bamboo, mountains, and water—continuing the ancient wisdom of "a home must have bamboo" while elevating it into a more complete and poetic way of life.

## Tips:

**Gudao Yuan**

Gudao Yuan is a perfect combination of the mountain dwellings in the Jiangnan region and modern aesthetics. The exterior wall features the traditional Chinese rammed earth structure, and the interior retains a large amount of original log structure. At the same time, there are overhanging balconies and large floor-to-ceiling windows. The overall style is simple and natural, echoing the mountains and forests, yet it stands out in the environment and catches people's eyes.

Walking along the ancient path behind the homestay, you can find the origin of white tea — the White Tea Ancestor: a wild tea tree with a history of a hundred years.

Experience Activities: At Gudao Yuan, you can not only climb the ancient path to search for the White Tea Ancestor, but also go rafting at the entrance of Daxi Village. You can also visit the nearby Jiulongxia Scenic Area and Jiangnan Tianchi.

**Address:** Hengkengwu Natural Village, Daxi Village, Tianhuangping Town

## Kaichen Xixinlu

Xixinlu is nestled among the mountains and deep within the bamboo forests, with a tranquil environment. It combines the traditional flavor of Jiangnan with a modern and minimalist style. The white walls, green tiles, and double eaves complement the natural surroundings perfectly. The architectural structure of the guest rooms has been carefully designed by the designers from the China Academy of Art. It retains the original rammed earth wall structure and explores more combinations of the old-fashioned style with aspects such as architecture and aesthetics.

Experience Activities: The homestay provides fresh and original ecological ingredients. The large floor-to-ceiling windows offer an unobstructed view of the scenery outside. You can savor the delicious food while enjoying the beautiful scenery outside the window and indulging in the wonderful moments of time.

**Address:** No. 122Hengyuanli Natural Village, Henglu Village, Tianhuangping Town

## Yinchuanju

The birth of Yinchuanju stems from the owner's trip to Japan. The Japanese-style homestay he stayed in not only had an elegant environment but also was an excellent location to overlook the beautiful scenery of Mount Fuji. At that time, the owner thought in his heart that his hometown village was also built against the mountains, and it was in no way inferior to this place. Therefore, three years later, a homestay named "Yinchuanju" was added in Shanchuan Township, and there was also a new wonderful place for tourists to stay and admire the beautiful landscapes of Anji.

Experience Activities: The natural scenery around Yinchuanju Homestay is beautiful. You can overlook the canyon and mountains. You can also go creek tracing in the Jingkongli Grand Canyon and go cycling on the mountains.

Address: Zheshiling, Chuancun Village, Shanchuan Township

### Qijianfang • Shanchuan Rural Residence

The decoration style of Qijianfang is simple yet warm. All the windows face south, overlooking the bamboo sea. Here, you can stroll along the mountain paths, listen to the chirping of birds and the singing of insects, and feel the tranquility and harmony of nature. You can also sit on the terrace or in the courtyard of the homestay and savor a cup of fragrant tea. On the hillside behind the building, there is a Chinese yew tree which is said to be the largest one in Anji County. Remember to find some time to go and have a look.

Experience Activities: Enjoy the scenery on the terrace and taste tea in the teahouse. Nearby attractions include the China Great Bamboo Sea, Anji Xianlongxia Rafting, and Anji Lingxi Mountain Scenic Area.

Address: Meishitou Natural Village, Majialong Village, Shanchuan Township

Yunzhongxi • Hot Spring Resort Hotel

Yunzhongxi is located in a valley, surrounded by lush bamboo forests and clear streams. The hotel has 23 guest rooms, all of which have floor-to-ceiling windows facing the bamboo sea. The hot spring here is a major highlight. The hot spring water is clear and transparent, and there are multiple characteristic hot spring pools, such as herbal medicine hot spring pools and flower-scented hot spring pools, etc., for guests to choose according to their personal preferences.

Experience Activities: The 270° landscape suite is equipped with a double-deck swimming pool, audio-visual facilities, outdoor bonfire barbecue, etc. Nearby scenic areas include Jiangnan Tianchi and Zhebei Grand Canyon.

Address: Dushan Temple, Longwang Village, Shangshu Township

瀑布咖啡 余村源 YU CUN YUAN 听闻旅拍 TING WEN GU ZHUANG 茉丽童画

盛世余村 YOWANT 遥望科技 NPI 恩派 竹境 匠人·匠道

尚灵文化 SHANGLIN MEDIA 原力食品 原力食品 田野家 PIXEL

青绿造物 GREEN CREATION Artie Studio 文益社 果潮蜜兔 GUOCHAOMETOO 上元集团 SHANGYUAN GROUP

Return Lab 拾回二手循环实验室 绿城服务 GREENTOWN DN余村 GALAXY LIFE

庆渔堂 celefish 为天下百姓养好鱼 余村机器人创新基地 YUCUN ROBOT INNOVATION BASE MEi@YUCUN 绿乡运营

绿茵里 GREENLEA 余村国际潮玩体育赛事 余村国际山地越野跑赛事 bilibili

中国电影基金会 CHINA FILM FOUNDATION 中国建筑科学研究院 China Academy of Building Research NDi 山系森活

周末 周末酒店 大秀云集 GATHERING IN DAXIU OKKA 承影互联

**图书在版编目（CIP）数据**

你好，大余村 / 汪玉成主编 . -- 杭州 : 西泠印社出版社 , 2025. 6. -- ISBN 978-7-5508-4801-6

Ⅰ . K928.955.4

中国国家版本馆 CIP 数据核字第 2025UD3737 号

**你好，大余村**

汪玉成　主编

---

**责任编辑**　刘　韵　吕逸尔
**责任出版**　杨飞凤
**责任校对**　吴乐文
**出版发行**　西泠印社出版社
（杭州市西湖文化广场 32 号 5 楼　邮政编码 310014）
**经　　销**　全国新华书店
**印　　刷**　杭州现代彩色印刷有限公司
**开　　本**　787mm×1092mm　1/32
**字　　数**　280 千
**印　　张**　11
**印　　数**　0001—10000
**书　　号**　ISBN 978-7-5508-4801-6
**版　　次**　2025 年 6 月第 1 版 第 1 次印刷
**定　　价**　68.00 元

---